JOHN ADAMS
1735—1826

Chronology—Documents—Bibliographical Aids

Edited by

HOWARD F. BREMER

Professor of History
Briarcliff College

Oceana Publications, Inc.
Dobbs Ferry, N.Y.
1967

Library of Congress Catalog Card Number: 67-19493

PRINTED IN THE UNITED STATES OF AMERICA

ii

CONTENTS

BIBLIOGRAPHICAL AIDS

EDITOR'S FOREWORD

Every attempt has been made to cite the most accurate dates in this Chronology. Diaries, documents, and similar evidence have been used to determine the exact date. If, however, later scholarship has found such dates to be obviously erroneous, the more plausible date has been used. Should this Chronology be in conflict with other authorities, the student is urged to go back to original sources as well as to such competent scholars as Lyman H. Butterfield.

This is a research tool compiled primarily for the student. While it does make some judgments on the significance of the events, it is hoped that they are reasoned judgments based on a long acquaintance with American History.

Obviously, the very selection of events by any writer is itself a judgment.

The essence of these little books is in their making available some pertinent facts and key documents **plus** a critical bibliography which should direct the student to investigate for himself additional and/or contradictory material. The works cited may not always be available in small libraries, but neither are they usually the old, out of print, type of books often included in similar accounts. Documents in this volume are taken from: William MacDonald, **Select Documents of the History of the United States, 1776-1861,** and James D. Richardson, ed., **Messages and Papers of the Presidents.** Vol. 2: **Adams.** 1897.

CHRONOLOGY

CHRONOLOGY

1735

**October 30
(Old Style,
October 19)**

Born, Braintree (now Quincy), Massachusetts. Father: John Adams. Mother: Susanna Boylston Adams.

1740's

Attended schools in Braintree kept by Mrs. Belcher and by Mr. Joseph Cleverly.

1750

Entered Joseph Marsh's school in Braintree, preparing for college.

1751

Entered Harvard College with the idea of becoming a clergyman. His interest turned to the law.

1755

July 16

Graduated with B.A. degree from Harvard. Hired by the Reverend Thaddeus Maccarty to teach school in Worcester, Massachusetts.

August

Began to keep school in Worcester.

November 18

First entry in his **Diary**. A rather severe earthquake that day may have jolted him into the practice.

1756

August 21

Completed a contract with James Putnam of Worcester to study law under him for two years, continuing, meantime, to teach scyool.

1758

July 19

Argued successfully for his M.A. degree from Harvard.

October

Returned to Braintree from Worcester to practice law.

November 6

Admitted to the bar, and began practice before Inferior Court of Common Pleas in Boston.

1

1761

February 9   Notation in his **Diary** praised George III, who had become King of England in 1760, and called him a "Patriot King."

February   Heard arguments in the Paxton Case by James Otis about the illegality of the Writs of Assistance; recorded some fifty years later that "here this day the child Independence was born."

May 25   Father died.
Inherited Braintree property later known as John Quincy Adams Birthplace.

November   Admitted to practice in the Superior Court of Judicature. Rode court circuits until 1776.

1762

October   First known record of courtship correspondence with Abigail, daughter of Reverend William Smith of Weymouth, Massachusetts.

1763

February   Notation in **Diary** about a "caucas" in Boston attended by Samuel Adams. Samuel and John had the same great-grandfather, Joseph Adams of Braintree. The Boston caucuses were to become the Sons of Liberty.

July 18   Essay on agriculture appeared in **Boston Evening Post** and **Boston Gazette**, written by Adams but signed "Humphrey Ploughjogger."

1764

October 25   Married Abigail Smith and they took up residence in his house in Braintree.

1765

January   Joined a "Sodality" in Boston made up of lawyers to discuss the theory and practice of law.

March   Elected a surveyor of highways in Braintree.

July 14   First daughter was born, named Abigail second.

September 24   Wrote **Braintree Instructions** against the Stamp Act.

1766

January   Wrote letters signed "Clarendon" for the **Boston Gazette**

on American constitutional rights.

March 3   Elected selectman for Braintree.

1767

July 11   First son born, named John Quincy.

1768

April   Family moved to the "White House on Brattle Square" in Boston.

June   Turned down offer from his friend Jonathan Sewall, Attorney General for Massachusetts, to become Advocate General for the Crown.

June 10   John Hancock's sloop **Liberty** was seized in Boston harbor and Hancock charged with smuggling of wine. Successfully defended by Adams during the next winter, the case was dropped by the government March 26, 1769.

December 28 Susanna, second daughter, was born. Died February 4, 1770.

1769

May-June   Successfully defended Michael Corbet, and three others accused of killing a British naval officer.

1770

March 5   Boston Massacre. Adams, with Josiah Quincy, successfully defended the British commander of the soldiers involved, Captain Thomas Preston, in a trial held in October. This was an unpopular action, but a courageous one.

May 29   Second son, Charles, was born.

August 14   Attended meeting of 350 Sons of Liberty.

1772

September 15 Thomas Boylston, third son, born.

December   Successfully defended Ansell Nickerson in admirality court against charge of murder.

1773

January 4   First of eight articles appeared in the **Boston Gazette** opposing crown salaries for Superior Court judges.

May 25   Elected by the House of Representatives to the Governor's Council, but vetoed two days later by Governor Thomas Hutchinson.

December 16   Boston Tea Party received Adams' approval next day in **Diary** as having "a Dignity, a Majesty, a Sublimity" that he greatly admired. "The people should never rise, without doing something to be remembered—something notable and striking."

1774

May 25   Again elected to the Governor's Council and again negatived, this time by General Thomas Gage, who had arrived May 13 to relieve Hutchinson and enforce the Coercive Acts.

June 17   Elected a Massachusetts delegate to the Continental Congress.

August 10   Set out for Philadelphia with the rest of the committee: Thomas Cushing, Samuel Adams, and Robert Treat Paine. The First Continental Congress assembled September 5.

September 17   Described this day as the happiest of his life when Congress unanimously approved the Suffolk Resolves, supporting Massachusetts in her resistance to British policy.

October 26   Congress adjourned and Adams left two days later for Braintree.

December 2   Reelected with his three colleagues to the Continental Congress. John Hancock added to delegation, and was to become President of the Congress.

1775

April 26   Just a week after Lexington and Concord, left Braintree for Philadelphia, arriving May 10 for Second Continental Congress opening that day.

Friend Josiah Quincy died on return voyage from England where he had tried to explain the position of American patriots to the British Government.

June 15   Nominated George Washington for Commander-in-Chief of Continental Army.

July   Attacked John Dickinson's views on conciliation in letters intercepted and published by the British.

August   Returned to Braintree and was reelected to Continental Congress.

September 12   Arrived at Philadelphia for third session of Congress. Played important role in establishment of an American navy.

October   Appointed Chief Justice of Massachusetts by Provincial Assembly; resigned in February, 1777, without ever serving.

November 29   Appointed one of a five man secret "Committee on Foreign Correspondence" to solicit aid abroad.

December   Returned to Braintree on leave from Congress; consulted with General Washington at Cambridge.

1776

January 9   Thomas Paine's **Common Sense** appeared unsigned and many believed Adams to be its author.

**February-
October**   Attended Continental Congress. Wrote **Thoughts on Government,** published by Richard Henry Lee, an important source for many state constitutions.

May 15   Helped draft a resolution stating that Great Britain's rule had come to an end in the colonies.

June 11   Appointed to the committee to prepare a Declaration of Independence, with Thomas Jefferson, Benjamin Franklin, Robert Livingston, and Roger Sherman.

June 12   Appointed to a committee to prepare a plan of treaties with foreign powers.

June 14   Congress assigned the "Committee on Spies," of which Adams was a member, the task of revising "the rules and articles of war."

June 15   Appointed president of the Board of War and Ordinance.

June 28   Draft of Declaration, written by Jefferson, with some changes by Adams and Franklin, submitted to Congress.

July 2   Voted for Lee's resolution declaring independence. The Declaration, amended this day and the next, was approved without dissent on July 4.

September 11   With Benjamin Franklin and Edward Rutledge, a committee appointed by Congress, held a fruitless "peace" conference with Admiral Lord Howe on Staten Island.

October 13   Obtained leave from Congress and returned to Braintree.

November 15   Reelected to Congress.

1777

January 9   Left for Baltimore, where Congress was now convening, by circuitous backcountry route.

**March-
September**   Attended Congress, which returned to Philadelphia on March 4.

September 19   Fled Philadelphia after the Battle of Brandywine with rest of Congress to Lancaster and then to York, arriving there on September 30.

October 14   Last major problem of Articles of Confederation solved. The articles were formally adopted on November 15, but not completely ratified by the states until March 1, 1781.

November 11   Obtained leave of absence from Congress and returned to Braintree where he resumed his law practice.

November 28   Appointed member of commission to France, with Franklin and Arthur Lee, to replace Silas Deane.

1778

February 13   Sailed with son, John Quincy, for Bordeaux. Treaties of Commerce and Alliance with France had been signed in Paris a week before.

April 1   Landed at Bordeaux after a voyage his **Diary** records in detail as tumultuous and dangerous.   •

Joined Franklin's household in Paris.

May 8   Received in audience by Louis XVI of France.

September 11   Congress voted to replace the commission in France with a minister, and named Franklin to the position. Adams had recommended this action.

1779

February 12 Wrote Count Vergennes, the French Foreign Minister, attacking Silas Deane and defending Arthur Lee, claiming that Franklin had been wrong in his judgments of these men.
Same day received word from America of appointment of Franklin as sole minister.

June 17 Sailed from Lorient on French frigate **La Sensible.** Arrived in Boston August 3.

August 9-
November 11 Major, if not sole, draftsman of a new state constitution for Massachusetts, adopted in 1780.

November 15 Sailed for Spain accompanied by John Quincy and Charles, having been commissioned by Congress to negotiate treaties of peace and commerce with Great Britain.

December 8 Arrived at Ferrol, Spain. Traveled in Spain during December and January. Spain was at war with Great Britain (since June 21) but not allied with the United States.

1780

February 9 Arrived in Paris.

June 20 Commissioned by Congress to try to negotiate a loan in the Netherlands.

July 27 Before learning of his commission, left Paris for Amsterdam as a private citizen, hoping to secure financial aid for America.

December 29 Adams instructed by Congress to attempt to negotiate a treaty with The Hague. Great Britain had broken relations with the Netherlands on December 21.

1781

June 11 Congress decided to add other names than Adams to commission to negotiate peace with Great Britain: John Jay, Benjamin Franklin, Henry Laurens and Thomas Jefferson added, the last named refusing the commission.

July 11 Met Vergennes at Versailles to discuss peace mediation attempts by Russia and Austria, with Vergennes apparently ready to compromise France's pledge of fighting until America gained Independence. Spurned Vergennes and returned to Amsterdam.

1782

April 19   Recognized by the Netherlands as minister plenipotentiary of the United States and established our first legation at The Hague.

June 11   Secured a loan of about $3,500,000 from a syndicate of Dutch bankers.

October 8   Signed at the Hague a treaty of amity and commerce.

November 30   In Paris signed, with Franklin and Jay, a preliminary treaty of peace with Britain negotiator Richard Oswald.

1783

September 3   Signed, with fellow commissioners, the definitive peace treaty with Great Britain.

October 20   After a serious illness left France for England, and to Bath for "the cure."

1784

March 9   Arranged a second loan in the Netherlands, the credit of the United States being in great jeopardy.

May 7   Appointed, with Franklin and Jefferson, to negotiate treaties with twenty-three nations. John Jay was elected secretary for foreign affairs, replacing Robert R. Livingston.

August 7   Abigail and daughter arrived in London from America and the Adams were reunited after a separation of over four years.

1785

February 24   Appointed first American minister to the Court of St. James. Shortly afterward (March 10) Jefferson named to succeed Franklin as minister to France.

May 21   John Quincy Adams sailed for America to enter Harvard.

June 1   Received by George III.

June 9	Leased house on Grosvenor Square as the first United States legation in London.
August 5	Signed treaty of amity and commerce with Prussia, Franklin and Jefferson having signed it in July.

1786

March-April	Jefferson visited Adams to attempt commercial treaties with Great Britain, Portugal, and Tripoli. The two traveled through English countryside.
June 11	Daughter Abigail married William Stephens Smith, American secretary at the legation, in London.

1787

January	First volume published in London of **A Defence of the Constitution of the United States of America:** the second volume in September, and the third the following year.
June 1	Negotiated third Dutch loan to the United States.
October 5	Congress voted to grant Adams' wish for recall, effective February, 1788.

1788

February 20	Granted final audience with George III.
March 13	Negotiated a fourth loan in Amsterdam.
March 30	With Abigail left London for America, arriving in Boston Harbor June 17 where several thousand people welcomed his return after nine years abroad.
June 18	Informed of his election (June 6) to the first Congress under the new Constitution. Never served, being elected Vice-President.

1789

April 6	Declared by Senate elected Vice-President, receiving 34 of the 69 votes.
April 21	Took seat as Vice-President and presided over Senate for next eight years.
June 3	Took oath of office and in turn administered the oath to members of the Senate.

1790

April   Contributed "Discourses on Davila" to John Fenno's **Gazette of the United States** until April, 1791.

1791

May   Elected president of the American Academy of Arts and Sciences, whose founding he had proposed twelve years earlier. Served until 1813.

May-
August   Opposed Jefferson's endorsement of Paine's **Rights of Man.**

1792

December 5   Reelected Vice-President, receiving 77 votes to the 50 cast for the Antifederalist George Clinton of New York.

1796

December 7   Presidential election held, with results in some doubt, although Adams seemed elected.

1797

February 8   Presided over Senate as votes for President and Vice-President were officially counted. Adams received 71, one more than the necessary majority of 70. Thomas Jefferson, Democratic-Republican, received 68 and was declared Vice-President. Thomas Pinckney, a Federalist, received 59 votes and Aaron Burr, Democratic-Republican, 20 votes. The remainder of the 276 votes was scattered over nine candidates.

TERM IN OFFICE

1797

March 4   Inaugurated as second president of the United States in the chamber of the House of Representatives in Philadelphia. Chief Justice Oliver Ellsworth administered the oath of office. Jefferson was sworn in as Vice-President, and Washington attended as a private citizen. Abigail was not present. The inaugural address was relatively short, and contained a plea for national unity—an obvious reference to the party strife which had developed.

All members of Adams' Cabinet carried over from the Washington administration: Secretary of State Timothy Pickering of Pennsylvania, Secretary of the Treasury Oliver Wolcott, Jr., of Connecticut, Secretary of War James McHenry of Maryland, Attorney General Charles Lee of Virginia, and Postmaster General Joseph Habersham of Georgia. Only Wolcott offered his resignation and it was not accepted.

March 11   Benjamin Franklin Bache, grandson of Franklin, praised Adams' Inaugural Address in his Republican newspaper, **The Aurora.** Bache usually delivered scurrilous attacks on Adams, as well as on George Washington.

April 17   Death of mother, Susanna (Boylston) Adams Hall.

May 10   First vessel of permanent navy, **United States,** launched at Philadelphia, with John Barry its commander.

May 16   Called special session of Congress and reported on French refusal to accept Charles Cotesworth Pinckney as minister to France in the preceding December. Told Congress of willingness to negotiate with France, but recommended defense measures.

May 31   Appointed commission to France including Pinckney plus John Marshall of Virginia, a Federalist, and Elbridge Gerry of Massachusetts, a Republican. Instructed commission to secure a treaty of commerce and amity.

**July-
August**   Spent summer in Quincy.

July 26   John Quincy Adams married Louisa Catherine Johnson in London. She was the daughter of the American consul.

August 28   Treaty with Tunis signed in Tunis. Not ratified by Adams until January 10, 1800.

September 7   Frigate **Constellation** launched at Baltimore, Maryland.

**October-
November**   Returned with wife from Quincy to Philadelphia.

October 4   Marshall, Pinckney, and Gerry arrived at Paris.

October 18   XYZ affair began when American commissioners were visited by three agents of Talleyrand, the French foreign minister, demanding a loan to France and a bribe of $240,000. The three Frenchmen were later designated as X, Y, and Z. Pinckney's answer was "No! No! Not a sixpence."

October 21   The **Constitution,** "Old Ironsides," launched in Boston.

November 23   Delivered first Annual Message to Congress, largely concerned with the crisis in relations with France.

December   Republicans launched attack on Adams' diplomacy. Thomas Jefferson, James Madison, James Monroe and Albert Gallatin wrote and spoke against the administration.

1798

January 8   Informed Congress that 11th Amendment had been adopted, providing that one state is not suable by citizens of another state. The decision in **Chisholm v. Georgia** (1793) led to the first change in the Constitution since the Bill of Rights.

February 1   Hamilton wrote Secretary of War McHenry that both navy and army should be strengthened. Secretary of State Pickering also favored a strong army, and so suggested to Adams, who rejected the idea.

February 22   Refused to attend a ball celebrating the birthday of George Washington. Abigail wrote that the President could not attend "in a secondary character."

March 12   Nominated son, John Quincy, commissioner to negotiate Treaty of Amity and Commerce with Sweden.

March 19   Reported to Congress on the failure of negotiations in France; declared the existence of a state of quasi-war with France.

March 27-
July 16   Series of defense measures enacted by Congress.

March 30   William Branch Giles, Republican Congressman from Virginia, demanded that the XYZ correspondence be released by the president; an attempt to show that the problems were not serious backfired for the Republicans.

April 3   Upon official request by the House, Adams released and published the XYZ papers, arousing American public opinion in both parties.

April 7   Mississippi Territory established.

April 25	First rendition of Joseph Hopkinson's "Hail Columbia."
April 30	Navy Department created by law of Congress.
May 21	Benjamin Stoddert of Maryland named Secretary of the Navy.
May 28	Authorized by Congress to raise an army of 10,000 volunteers.
June 13	Congress suspended trade with France and her colonies.
June 18	Naturalization Act extended from 5 to 14 years the required time of residence for citizenship. Restored to 5 years in 1802.
	Robert Goodloe Harper, Congressman from Virginia, in a toast used the phrase "Millions for defense but not a cent for tribute."
June 21	Message to Congress stated that no more ministers would be sent to France without assurance of a respectful reception; the message avoided extreme language.
June 22	Authorized by Congress to appoint commissioned officers for the 10,000 man army and wrote Washington that same day requesting him to be its commander-in-chief.
June 25	Alien Act gave the President authority to expel aliens dangerous to the public safety or suspected of treasonable tendencies. The Act expired in 1802.
July 2	Nominated George Washington Commander-in-Chief of the Army. Confirmed by Senate July 3.
July 4	Washington demanded that he have the right to recommend his general staff officers and insisted on Hamilton as his second in command over Henry Knox or Charles Cotesworth Pinckney. For weeks the issue brought angry exchanges of letters: Knox refused to serve under Hamilton, Adams supported Knox, Washington seemingly about to resign, Hamilton insisting on second rank.
July 6	Alien Enemies Act passed, calling for the removal of persons of that description in time of war.

July 7   Congress repealed the alliance with France of 1778.

July 9   Evaluation Act ("Window Tax") passed on this date and July 14, providing direct taxes on land, houses, and slaves.

July 11   The Marine Corps established by Congress.

July 14   Sedition Act passed, providing fines and imprisonment for persons conspiring against the government and its laws, for attempting or aiding "insurrections, riots or unlawful assembly," and for "false, scandalous and malicious" writing or utterances against the government. Remained in force until March 3, 1801.
Adams signed the bill, but was not active in its enforcement. Others of his cabinet were, particularly Timothy Pickering. Undoubtedly aimed at suppressing political opposition, it resulted in the indictment of about fifteen persons of whom ten were convicted.

**July 25-
November 20** On or about these dates Adams left and returned to Philadelphia spending the time in Quincy. He left without notifying either Pickering or McHenry. Abigail was seriously ill during this period.

September 10 Death of Benjamin Franklin Bache prevented trial for libel by a federal court.

September 30 Commissioned Henry Knox, Charles Cotesworth Pinckney, and Alexander Hamilton major generals without deciding their relative rank.

October 1 Elbridge Gerry arrived in Boston and went straight to Quincy to report to Adams that France wanted peace as quickly as possible.

October 2 Signed treaty with Cherokee Indians.

October 9 Yielded to Washington on Hamilton's rank as second in command, a humiliating defeat for Adams.

November 16 Kentucky Resolutions, drafted by Jefferson in reaction against the Alien and Sedition Acts, passed by the state legislature on this date and on November 22.

November 20 Undeclared naval war with France began with the capture of the schooner **Retaliation** by the French off Guadeloupe.

December 8 Delivered second Annual Message to Congress, a conciliatory one, suggesting a new mission to France.

December 24 Virginia Resolutions, drafted by Madison, like the Kentucky Resolutions declared the Alien and Sedition Acts to be unconstitutional.

1799

January 30 "Logan" Act passed, prohibiting private diplomacy. Dr. George Logan, a Pennsylvania Quaker, had gone to France in 1798 on his own responsibility to try to bring about better relations. Both President Adams and George Washington received him with coolness upon his return in November, and the Federalists in Congress were especially angered by his assertions in the press of France's peaceful intentions.

February The Fries Rebellion broke out in Eastern Pennsylvania, an uprising led by John Fries in opposition to the property taxes of July 9 and 14, 1798. Adams called on the militia and regular army to march against the rebels. Fries, convicted of treason and sentenced to death, was pardoned by President Adams.

February 9 The **Constitution,** commanded by Commodore Thomas Truxton, captured the French frigate **L'Insurgante** off Nevis; the first test of battle for the new navy.

February 18 Nominated William Vans Murray as minister to France after receiving word that an American would be received with respect. Done without consultation with his cabinet, the move was a surprise and blow to the Hamilton pro-war faction.

February 25 The Senate refusing to confirm a single emissary, Adams nominated Murray, Patrick Henry and Chief Justice Oliver Ellsworth as ministers plenipotentiary to France. Patrick Henry, declining because of age, was replaced by Governor William R. Davie of North Carolina.

March 11-
October 10 Absent from capital, spending period at home in Quincy. Probably avoiding his uncooperative cabinet, was sub-

jected to much criticism for his prolonged vacation. But Abigail was ill, and he was having tooth trouble.

June 29   Thomas Cooper printed a scathing attack on Adams in the **Northumberland Gazette** (Philadelphia). Brought to trial for libel, was sentenced to six month's imprisonment.

October 10 Returned to capital, then in Trenton, New Jersey, because of yellow fever epidemic in Philadelphia.

October 16 Issued order for the departure of Ellsworth and Davie to join Murray, already in France. Pickering had stalled on the action throughout the summer.

December 3 6th Congress organized with a Federalist majority. Adams' Annual Message urged peace and an end to civil disturbances.

December 14 George Washington died.

1800

March 8   Napoleon respectfully received American commissioners.

April 4   Federal Bankruptcy Act signed enabling Robert Morris to be freed from prison.

April 24   Signed law establishing the Library of Congress.

May   Caucuses in Congress renominated Adams for a second term.

May 5   Accused Secretary of War McHenry of faults and failures to cooperate.

May 6   McHenry resigned, effective May 31.

May 10   Requested resignation of Secretary of State Pickering, who, not choosing to resign, was dismissed May 12.

May 13   Appointed John Marshall of Virginia as Secretary of State; assumed duties June 6.
Appointed Samuel Dexter of Massachusetts as Secretary of War; assumed duties June 12.

June 30-
November 1 Spent in Quincy.

September 30 Treaty of Morfontaine, often called Convention of 1800, signed in Paris with Napoleon. Released the United States from the Alliance of 1778, and ended the quasi-war with France.

October 1 France regained Louisiana from Spain in a secret agreement.

October Hamilton circulated a bitter, illogical attack on Adams to the inner circle of Federalists. Later published as **Letter Concerning the Public Conduct and Character of John Adams.**

November 1 Arrived in Washington, soon followed by Abigail, to become first occupants of the still unfinished White House.

November 17 First session of Congress to convene in Washington.

November 22 Read fourth Annual Message to Congress.

November 30 Charles, second son, died in New York City.

December 3 Defeated for reelection, both Thomas Jefferson and Aaron Burr receiving 73 electoral votes to Adams' 65.

1801

January 20 Appointed John Marshall as Chief Justice of the Supreme Court. Approved by Senate January 27.

January 31 Instructed John Marshall to order the return of John Quincy Adams from his post as minister to Prussia to prevent his dismissal by President-elect Jefferson.

February 13 Judiciary Act signed reducing the number of Supreme Court justices to 5 and establishing 16 circuit courts. Used by Adams and the Federalists for political purposes made the "midnight appointments," a group of Federalist judges and court officials. Repealed March 8, 1802.

March 2 Appointed William Marbury a justice of the peace for the District of Columbia, setting the stage for the famous **Marbury v. Madison** case in 1803 after President Jefferson had ordered his Secretary of State to withhold the appointment.

March 3 Signed last of "midnight appointments" at 9 P.M., naming Hugh Barclay a marshal in Pennsylvania. Also appointed the first faculty members to a school for gunners and sappers at West Point, destined to become the United States Military Academy in 1802.

RETIREMENT
1801
March 4   Refused to attend the inauguration of Jefferson, leaving Washington early that morning for Quincy.

1802
September 4 John Quincy Adams and wife arrived in Philadelphia from Berlin, and traveled to Quincy.

October 5   Began writing his **Autobiography**, completing Part One, "John Adams," in June, 1805.

1806
December 1   Began Part Two of **Autobiography**, "Travels, and Negotiations," which he never finished. Part Three, "Peace," written in 1807, is also incomplete.

1807
July 11   Began controversy with Mercy Otis Warren about her **History.**

1809
April 10   Began a series of 130 letters to the **Boston Patriot,** a Jeffersonian paper, published from April 15 until May, 1812. These self-justifying letters are referred to as his "second autobiography."

April 19-
May 3   Published four letters on foreign policy in the **Patriot.**

1812
January   Resumed correspondence with Thomas Jefferson through the intercession of Dr. Benjamin Rush. Adams and Rush had long carried on a correspondence.

1813
August 14   Death of daughter, Abigail Adams Smith.

1817
March 5   Son, John Quincy Adams, appointed Secretary of State by President James Monroe.

1818
October 28   Death of wife, Abigail Smith Adams.

1820

November-
December Attended Massachusetts Constitutional Convention as delegate from Quincy.

1822

June-
August Provided funds for a church and an academy in Quincy, and gave his library to the academy. The academy was never established and Adams' library finally was housed in the Boston Public Library.

1824

December 1 Presidential election held with son, John Quincy Adams, receiving a minority of the votes cast.

1825

February 9 John Quincy Adams elected President by the House of Representatives.

1826

July 4 Death occurred at Quincy. Not knowing that Thomas Jefferson had died a few hours earlier, Adams' last words were said to be "Thomas Jefferson still survives."

DOCUMENTS

JOHN ADAMS ON INDEPENDENCE
May 17, 1776

Adams, with Edward Rutledge and Richard Henry Lee, had drafted a resolution adopted by Congress on May 15 stating that Great Britain's rule had come to an end in America. The resolution recommended that colonial government be established which should "best conduce to the happiness and safety" of Americans. Adams wrote a letter to his wife Abigail two days later, excerpts from which follow (Letters of John Adams to His Wife, I, 109-111).

I have this morning heard Mr. Duffield, upon the signs of the times . . . . He concluded, that the course of events indicated strongly the design of Providence, that we should be separated from Great Britain, etc. . . .

It it not a saying of Moses, "who am I, that I should go in and out before this great people?" When I consider the great events which are passed, and those greater which are rapidly advancing, and that I may have been instrumental in touching some springs, and turning some small wheels, which have had and will have such effects, I feel an awe upon my mind, which is not easily described. Great Britain has at last driven America to the last step, a complete separation from her; a total absolute independence, not only of her Parliament, but of her crown, **for such is the amount of the resolve of the 15th. Confederation among ourselves, or alliances with foreign nations, are not necessary to a perfect separation from Britain. That is effected by extinguishing all authority under the crown, Parliament, and nation, as the resolution for instituting governments has done, to all intents and purposes.** Confederation will be necessary for our internal concord, and alliances may be so for our external defence.

I have reasons to believe that no colony, which shall assume a government under the people, will give it up. There is something very unnatural and odious in a government a thousand leagues off. A whole government of our own choice, managed by persons whom we love, revere, and can confide in, has charms in it, for which men will fight.

Two young gentlemen from South Carolina in this city, who were in Charlestown when their new constitution was promulgated, and when their new Governor and Council and Assembly walked out in procession, attended by the guards, company of cadets, light horse, etc., told me, that they were beheld by the people with transports and tears of joy. The people gazed at them with a kind of rapture. They both told me, that the reflection, that these were gentlemen whom they all loved, esteemed and revered, gentlemen of their own choice, whom they could trust, and whom they could displace, if any of them should behave amiss, affected them so, that they could not help crying. **They say, their people will never give up this government.** . . .

JOHN ADAMS ON OCHLOCRACY
1776

Adams feared "ochlocracy," or government by the crowd or mob. He even severely rebuked his wife for suggesting that the Revolution might do something about women's rights. In his **Autobiography (Works, II, 420-421)** *he worried about giving power to the "debtor" class.*

An event of the most trifling nature in appearance, and fit only to excite laughter in other times, struck me into a profound reverie, if not a fit of melancholy. I met a man who had sometimes been my client, and sometimes I had been against him. He, though a common horse-jocky, was sometimes in the right, and I had commonly been successful in his favor in our courts of law. He was always in the law, and had been sued in many actions at almost every court. As soon as he saw me, he came up to me, and his first salutation to me was, "Oh! Mr. Adams, what great things have you and your colleagues done for us! We can never be grateful enough to you. There are no courts of justice now in this Province and I hope there never will be another." Is this the object for which I have been contending? said I to myself, for I rode along without any answer to this wretch. Are these the sentiments of such people, and how many of them are there in the country? Half the nation, for what I know; for half the nation are debtors, if not more, and these have been, in all countries, the sentiments of debtors. If the power of the country should get into such hands, and there is great danger that it will, to what purpose have we sacrificed our time, health and every thing else? Surely we must guard against this spirit and these principles, or we shall repent of all our conduct. However, the good sense and integrity of the majority of the great body of the people came into my thoughts, for my relief, and the last resource was after all in a good Providence.

INAUGURAL ADDRESS
Philadelphia, Pa.
March 4, 1797

Adams' Inaugural Address was delivered in the Senate Chamber of Congress Hall before both houses of Congress. Adams, in contrast with his usual simple dress, wore a pearl-colored broadcloth suit, a sword and cockade. George Washington was there, undoubtedly the center of attraction, and, as Adams described it: "A solemn scene it was indeed, and it was made affecting to me by the presence of the General, whose countenance was as serene and unclouded as the day. He seemed to me to enjoy a triumph over me. Methought I heard him say, 'Ay! I am fairly out and you fairly in! See which of us will be happiest!'" The eulogy of Washington in the speech was apparently at odds with Adams' real convictions. Adams' support of the Constitution and his political philosophy are expressed in one gargantuan sentence toward the end of the address.

When it was first perceived, in early times, that no middle course for America remained between unlimited submission to a foreign legislature and a total independence of its claims, men of reflection were less apprehensive of danger from the formidable power of fleets and armies they must determine to resist than from those contests and dissensions which would certainly arise concerning the forms of government to be instituted over the whole and over the parts of this extensive country. Relying, however, on the purity of their intentions, the justice of their cause, and the integrity and intelligence of the people, under an overruling Providence which had so signally protected this country from the first, the representatives of this nation, then consisting of little more than half its present number, not only broke to pieces the chains which were forging and the rod of iron that was lifted up, but frankly cut asunder the ties which had bound them, and launched into an ocean of uncertainty.

The zeal and ardor of the people during the Revolutionary war, supplying the place of government, commanded a degree of order sufficient at least for the temporary preservation of society. The Confederation which was early felt to be necessary was prepared from the models of the Batavian and Helvetic confederacies, the only examples which remain with any detail and precision in history, and certainly the only ones which the people at large had ever considered. But reflecting on the striking difference in so many particulars between this country and those where a courier may go from the seat of government to the frontier in a single day, it was then certainly foreseen by some who assisted in Congress at the formation of it that it could not be durable.

Negligence of its regulations, inattention to its recommendations, if not disobedience to its authority, not only in individuals but in States, soon appeared with their melancholy consequences—universal languor, jealousies and rivalries of States, decline of navigation and commerce, discouragement of necessary manufactures, universal fall in the value of lands and their produce, contempt of public and private faith, loss of consideration and credit with foreign nations, and at length in discontents, animosities, combinations, partial conventions, and insurrection, threatening some great national calamity.

In this dangerous crisis the people of America were not abandoned by their usual good sense, presence of mind, resolution, or integrity. Measures were pursued to concert a plan to form a more perfect union, establish justice, insure domestic tranquillity, provide for the common defense, promote the general welfare, and secure the blessings of liberty. The public disquisitions, discussions, and deliberations issued in the present happy Constitution of Government.

Employed in the service of my country abroad during the whole course of these transactions, I first saw the Constitution of the United States in a foreign country. Irritated by no literary altercation, animated by no public debate, heated by no party animosity, I read it with great satisfaction, as the result of good heads.prompted by good hearts, as an experiment better adapted to the genius, character, situation, and relations of this nation and country than any which had ever been proposed or suggested. In its general principles and great outlines it was conformable to such a system of government as I had ever most esteemed, and in some States, my own native State in particular, had contributed to establish. Claiming a right of suffrage, in common with my fellow-citizens, in the adoption or rejection of a constitution which was to rule me and my posterity, as well as them and theirs, I did not hesitate to express my approbation of it on all occasions, in public and in private. It was not then, nor has been since, any objection to it in my mind that the Executive and Senate were not more permanent. Nor have I ever entertained a thought of promoting any alteration in it but such as the people themselves, in the course of their experience, should see and feel to be necessary or expedient, and by their representatives in Congress and the State legislatures, according to the Constitution itself, adopt and ordain.

Returning to the bosom of my country after a painful separation from it for ten years, I had the honor to be elected to a station under the new order of things, and I have repeatedly laid myself under the most serious obligations to support the Constitution. The operations of it has equaled the most sanguine expectations of its friends, and from an habitual attention to it, satisfaction in its administration, and delight in its effects upon the peace, order, prosperity, and happiness of the nation I have acquired an habitual attachment to it and veneration for it.

What other form of government, indeed, can so well deserve our esteem and love?

There may be little solidity in an ancient idea that congregations of men into cities and nations are the most pleasing objects in the sight of superior intelligences, but this is very certain, that to a benevolent human mind there can be no spectacle presented by any nation more pleasing, more noble, majestic, or august, than an assembly like that which has so often been seen in this and the other Chamber of Congress, of a Government in which the Executive authority, as well as that of all the branches of the Legislature, are exercised by citizens selected at regular periods by their neighbors to make and execute laws for the general good. Can anything essential, anything more than mere ornament and decoration, be added to this by robes and diamonds? Can authority be more amiable and respectable when it descends from accidents or institutions established in remote antiquity than when it springs fresh from the hearts and judgments of an honest and enlightened people? For it is the people only that are represented. It is their power and majesty that is reflected, and only for their good, in every legitimate government, under whatever form it may appear. The existence of such a government as ours for any length of time is a full proof of a general dissemination of knowledge and virtue throughout the whole body of the people. And what object or consideration more pleasing than this can be presented to the human mind? If national pride is ever justifiable or excusable it is when it springs, not from power or riches, grandeur or glory, but from conviction of national innocence, information, and benevolence.

In the midst of these pleasing ideas we should be unfaithful to ourselves if we should ever lose sight of the danger to our liberties if anything partial or extraneous should infect the purity of our free, fair, virtuous, and independent elections. If an election is to be determined by a majority of a single vote, and that can be procured by a party through artifice or corruption, the Government may be the choice of a party for its own ends, not of the nation for the national good. If that solitary suffrage can be obtained by foreign nations by flattery or menaces, by fraud or violence, by terror, intrigue, or venality, the Government may not be the choice of the American people, but of foreign nations. It may be foreign nations who govern us, and not we, the people, who govern ourselves; and candid men will acknowledge that in such cases choice would have little advantage to boast of over lot or chance.

Such is the amiable and interesting system of government (and such are some of the abuses to which it may be exposed) which the people of America have exhibited to the admiration and anxiety of the wise and virtuous of all nations for eight years under the administration of a citizen who, by a long course of great actions, regulated by prudence, justice, temperance, and fortitude, conducting a people inspired with the same virtues and animated with the same ardent patriotism and love of liberty to independence and peace, to increasing wealth and unexampled prosperity, has merited the gratitude of his fellow-citizens, commanded the highest praises of foreign nations, and secured immortal glory with posterity.

In that retirement which is his voluntary choice may he long live to enjoy the delicious recollection of his services, the gratitude of mankind, the happy fruits of them to himself and the world, which are daily increasing, and that splendid prospect of the future fortunes of this country which is opening from year to year. His name may be still a rampart, and the knowledge that he lives a bulwark, against all open or secret enemies of his country's peace. This example has been recommended to the imitation of his successors by both Houses of Congress and by the voice of the legislatures and the people throughout the nation.

On this subject it might become me better to be silent or to speak with diffidence; but as something may be expected the occasion, I hope, will be admitted as an apology if I venture to say that if a preference, upon principle, of a free republican government, formed upon long and serious reflection, after a diligent and impartial inquiry after truth; if an attachment to the Constitution of the United States, and a conscientious determination to support it until it shall be altered by the judgments and wishes of the people, expressed in the mode prescribed in it; if a respectful attention to the constitutions of the individual States and a constant caution and delicacy toward the State governments; if an equal and impartial regard to the rights, interest, honor, and happiness of all the States in the Union, without preference or regard to a northern or southern, an eastern or western, position, their various political opinions on unessential points or their personal attachments; if a love of virtuous men of all parties and denominations; if a love of science and letters and a wish to patronize every rational effort to encourage schools, colleges, universities, academies, and every institution for propagating knowledge, virtue, and religion among all classes of the people, not only for their benign influence on the happiness of life in all its stages and classes, and of society in all its forms, but as the only means of preserving our Constitution from its natural enemies, the spirit of sophistry, the spirit of party, the spirit of intrigue, the profligacy of corruption, and the pestilence of foreign influence, which is the angel of destruction to elective governments; if a love of equal laws, of justice, and humanity in the interior administration; if an inclination to improve agriculture, commerce, and manufactures for necessity, convenience, and defense; if a spirit of equity and humanity toward the aboriginal nations of America, and a disposition to meliorate their condition by inclining them to be more friendly to us, and our citizens to be more friendly to them; if an inflexible determination to maintain peace and inviolable faith with all nations, and that system of neutrality and impartiality among the belligerent powers of Europe which has been adopted by this Government and so solemnly sanctioned by both Houses of Congress and applauded by the legislatures of the States and the public opinion, until it shall be otherwise ordained by Congress; if a personal esteem for the French nation, formed in a residence of seven years chiefly among them, and a sincere desire to preserve the friendship which has been so much for the honor and interest of both nations; if, while the conscious honor and integrity of the people of America and the internal sentiment of their own power and energies must be preserved, an earnest endeavor to investigate every just cause and remove every colorable pretense of complaint; if an intention to pursue by amicable negotiation a reparation for the injuries that have been committed on the commerce of our fellow-citizens by whatever nation, and if success can not be obtained, to lay the facts before the Legislature, that they may consider what further measures the honor and interest of the Government and its constituents demand; if a resolution to do justice as far as may depend upon me, at all times and to all nations, and maintain peace, friendship, and benevolence with all the world; if an unshaken confidence in the honor, spirit, and resources of the American people, on which I have so often hazarded my all and never been deceived; if elevated ideas of the high destinies of this country and of my own duties toward it, founded on a knowledge of the moral principles and intellectual improvements of the people deeply engraven on my mind in early life, and not obscured but exalted by experience and age; and, with humble reverence, I feel it to be my duty to add, if a veneration for the religion of a people who profess and call themselves Christians, and a fixed resolution to consider a decent respect for Christianity among the best recommendations for the public service, can enable me in any degree to comply with your wishes, it shall be my strenuous endeavor that this sagacious injunction of the two Houses shall not be without effect.

With this great example before me, with the sense and spirit, the faith and honor, the duty and interest, of the same American people pledged to support the Constitution of the United States, I entertain no doubt of its continuance in all its energy, and my mind is prepared without hesitation to lay myself under the most solemn obligations to support it to the utmost of my power.

And may that Being who is supreme over all, the Patron of Order, the Fountain of Justice, and the Protector in all ages of the world of virtuous liberty, continue His blessing upon this nation and its Government and give it all possible success and duration consistent with the ends of His providence.

MARCH 4, 1797.

SPECIAL SESSION MESSAGE
May 16, 1797

French refusal to accept Charles Cotsworth Pinckney
as minister from the United States and increasing
seizures of American ships led Adams to call a special
session of Congress. The call went out on March 25,
1797 to meet May 15, but it took two days to as-
semble a quorum. Hamilton and the High Federalists
wanted an army of 25,000 and increased taxes to sup-
port defense measures, and Adams in his speech seem-
ed to be in accord with these sentiments. Yet his aim
was undoubtedly to avoid war. The Republicans inter-
preted the speech, nevertheless, as a call for war.

UNITED STATES, May 16, 1797.
Gentlemen of the Senate and Gentlemen of the House of Representatives:

The personal inconveniences to the members of the Senate and of the House of Representatives in leaving their families and private affairs at this season of the year are so obvious that I the more regret the extraordinary occasion which has rendered the convention of Congress indispensable.

It would have afforded me the highest satisfaction to have been able to congratulate you on a restoration of peace to the nations of Europe whose animosities have endangered our tranquillity; but we have still abundant cause of gratitude to the Supreme Dispenser of National Blessings for general health and promising seasons, for domestic and social happiness, for the rapid progress and ample acquisitions of industry through extensive territories, for civil, political, and religious liberty. While other states are desolated with foreign war or convulsed with intestine divisions, the United States present the pleasing prospect of a nation governed by mild and equal laws, generally satisfied with the possession of their rights, neither envying the advantages nor fearing the power of other nations, solicitous only for the maintenance of order and justice and the preservation of liberty, increasing daily in their attachment to a system of government in proportion to their experience of its utility, yielding a ready and general obedience to laws flowing from the reason and resting on the only solid foundation—the affections of the people.

It is with extreme regret that I shall be obliged to turn your thoughts to other circumstances, which admonish us that some of these felicities may not be lasting. But if the tide of our prosperity is full and a reflux commencing, a vigilant circumspection becomes us, that we may meet our reverses with fortitude and extricate ourselves from their consequences with all the skill we possess and all the efforts in our power.

In giving to Congress information of the state of the Union and recommending to their consideration such measures as appear to me to be necessary or expedient, according to my constitutional duty, the causes and the objects of the present extraordinary session will be explained.

After the President of the United States received information that the French Government had expressed serious discontents at some proceedings of the Government of these States said to affect the interests of France, he thought it expedient to send to that country a new minister, fully instructed to enter on such amicable discussions and to give such candid explanations as might happily remove the discontents and suspicions of the French Government and vindicate the conduct of the United States. For this purpose he selected from among his fellow-citizens a character whose integrity, talents, experience, and services had placed him in the rank of the most esteemed and respected in the nation. The direct object of his mission was expressed in his letter of credence to the French Republic, being "to maintain that good understanding which from the commencement of the alliance had subsisted between the two nations, and to efface unfavorable impressions, banish suspicions, and restore that cordiality which was at once the evidence and pledge of a friendly union." And his instructions were to the same effect, "faithfully to represent the disposition of the Government and people of the United States (their disposition being one), to remove jealousies and obviate complaints by shewing that they were groundless, to restore that mutual confidence which had been so unfortunately and injuriously impaired, and to explain the relative interests of both countries and the real sentiments of his own."

A minister thus specially commissioned it was expected would have proved the instrument of restoring mutual confidence between the two Republics. The first step of the French Government corresponded with that expectation. A few days before his arrival at Paris the French minister of foreign relations informed the American minister then resident at Paris of the formalities to be observed by himself in taking leave, and by his successor preparatory to his reception. These formalities they observed, and on the 9th of December presented officially to the minister of foreign relations, the one a copy of his letters of recall, the other a copy of his letters of credence.

These were laid before the Executive Directory. Two days afterwards the minister of foreign relations informed the recalled American minister that the Executive Directory had determined not to receive another minister plenipotentiary from the United States until after the redress of grievances demanded of the American Government, and which the French Republic had a right to expect from it. The American minister immediately endeavored to ascertain whether by refusing to receive him it was intended that he should retire from the territories of the French Republic, and verbal answers were given that such was the intention of the Directory. For his own justification he desired a written answer, but obtained none until toward the last of January, when, receiving notice in writing to quit the territories of the Republic, he proceeded to Amsterdam, where he proposed to wait for instruction from this Government. During his residence at Paris cards of hospitality were refused him, and he was threatened with being subjected to the jurisdiction of the minister of police; but with becoming firmness he insisted on the protection of the law of nations due to him as the known minister of a foreign power. You will derive further information from his dispatches, which will be laid before you.

As it is often necessary that nations should treat for the mutual advantages of their affairs, and especially to accommodate and terminate differences, and as they can treat only by ministers, the right of embassy is well known and established by the law and usage of nations. The refusal on the part of France to receive our minister is, then, the denial of a right; but the refusal to receive him until we have acceded to their demands without discussion and without investigation is to treat us neither as allies nor as friends, nor as a sovereign state.

With this conduct of the French Government it will be proper to take into view the public audience given to the late minister of the United States on his taking leave of the Executive Directory. The speech of the President discloses sentiments more alarming than the refusal of a minister, because more dangerous to our independence and union, and at the same time studiously marked with indignities toward the Government of the United States. It evinces a disposition to separate the people of the United States from the Government, to persuade them that they have different affections, principles, and interests from those of their fellow-citizens whom they themselves have chosen to manage their common concerns, and thus to produce divisions fatal to our peace. Such attempts ought to be repelled with a decision which shall convince France and the world that we are not a degraded people, humiliated under a colonial spirit of fear and sense of inferiority, fitted to be the miserable instruments of foreign influence, and regardless of national honor, character, and interest.

I should have been happy to have thrown a veil over these transactions if it had been possible to conceal them; but they have passed on the great theater of the world, in the face of all Europe and America, and with such circumstances of publicity and solemnity that they can not be disguised and will not soon be forgotten. They have inflicted a wound in the American breast. It is my sincere desire, however, that it may be healed.

It is my sincere desire, and in this I presume I concur with you and with our constituents, to preserve peace and friendship with all nations; and believing that neither the honor nor the interest of the United States absolutely forbid the repetition of advances for securing these desirable objects with France, I shall institute a fresh attempt at negotiation, and shall not fail to promote and accelerate an accommodation on terms compatible with the rights, duties, interests, and honor of the nation. If we have committed errors, and these can be demonstrated, we shall be willing to correct them; if we have done injuries, we shall be willing on conviction to redress them; and equal measures of justice we have a right to expect from France and every other nation.

The diplomatic intercourse between the United States and France being at present suspended, the Government has no means of obtaining official information from that country. Nevertheless, there is reason to believe that the Executive Directory passed a decree on the 2d of March last contravening in part the treaty of amity and commerce of 1778, injurious to our lawful commerce and endangering the lives of our citizens. A copy of this decree will be laid before you.

While we are endeavoring to adjust all our differences with France by amicable negotiation, the progress of the war in Europe, the depredations on our commerce, the personal injuries to our citizens, and the general complexion of affairs render it my indispensable duty to recommend to your consideration effectual measures of defense.

The commerce of the United States has become an interesting object of attention, whether we consider it in relation to the wealth and finances or the strength and resources of the nation. With a seacoast of near 2,000 miles in extent, opening a wide field for fisheries, navigation, and commerce, a great portion of our citizens naturally apply their industry and enterprise to these objects. Any serious and permanent injury to commerce would not fail to produce the most embarrassing disorders. To prevent it from being undermined and destroyed it is essential that it receive an adequate protection.

The naval establishment must occur to every man who considers the injuries committed on our commerce, the insults offered to our citizens, and the description of vessels by which these abuses have been practiced. As the sufferings of our mercantile and seafaring citizens can not be ascribed to the omission of duties demandable, considering the neutral situation of our country, they are to be attributed to the hope of impunity arising from a supposed inability on our part to afford protection. To resist the consequences of such impressions on the minds of foreign nations and to guard against the degradation and servility which they must finally stamp on the American character is an important duty of Government.

A naval power, next to the militia, is the natural defense of the United States. The experience of the last war would be sufficient to shew that a moderate naval force, such as would be easily within the present abilities of the Union, would have been sufficient to have baffled many formidable transportations of troops from one State to another, which were then practiced. Our seacoasts, from their great extent, are more easily annoyed and more easily defended by a naval force than any other. With all the materials our country abounds; in skill our naval architects and navigators are equal to any, and commanders and seamen will not be wanting.

But although the establishment of a permanent system of naval defense appears to be requisite, I am sensible it can not be formed so speedily and extensively as the present crisis demands. Hitherto I have thought proper to prevent the sailing of armed vessels except on voyages to the East Indies, where general usage and the danger from pirates appeared to render the permission proper. Yet the restriction has originated solely from a wish to prevent collisions with the powers at war, contravening the act of Congress of June, 1794, and not from any doubt entertained by me of the policy and propriety of permitting our vessels to employ means of defense while engaged in a lawful foreign commerce. It remains for Congress to prescribe such regulations as will enable our seafaring citizens to defend themselves against violations of the law of nations, and at the same time restrain them from committing acts of hostility against the powers at war. In addition to this voluntary provision for defense by individual citizens, it appears to me necessary to equip the frigates, and provide other vessels of inferior force, to take under convoy such merchant vessels as shall remain unarmed.

The greater part of the cruisers whose depredations have been most injurious have been built and some of them partially equipped in the United States. Although an effectual remedy may be attended with difficulty, yet I have thought it my duty to present the subject generally to your consideration. If a mode can be devised by the wisdom of Congress to prevent the resources of the United States from being converted into the means of annoying our trade, a great evil will be prevented. With the same view, I think it proper to mention that some of our citizens resident abroad have fitted out privateers, and others have voluntarily taken the command, or entered on board of them, and committed spoliations on the commerce of the United States. Such unnatural and iniquitous practices can be restrained only by severe punishments.

But besides a protection of our commerce on the seas, I think it highly necessary to protect it at home, where it is collected in our most important ports. The distance of the United States from Europe and the well-known promptitude, ardor, and courage of the people in defense of their country happily diminish the probability of invasion. Nevertheless, to guard against sudden and predatory incursions the situation of some of our principal seaports demands your consideration. And as our country is vulnerable in other interests besides those of its commerce, you will seriously deliberate whether the means of general defense ought not to be increased by an addition to the regular artillery and cavalry, and by arrangements for forming a provisional army.

With the same view, and as a measure which, even in a time of universal peace, ought not to be neglected, I recommend to your consideration a revision of the laws for organizing, arming, and disciplining the militia, to render that natural and safe defense of the country efficacious.

Although it is very true that we ought not to involve ourselves in the political system of Europe, but to keep ourselves always distinct and separate from it if we can, yet to effect this separation, early, punctual, and continual information of the current chain of events and of the political projects in contemplation is no less necessary than if we were directly concerned in them. It is necessary, in order to the discovery of the efforts made to draw us into the vortex, in season to make preparations against them. However we may consider ourselves, the maritime and commercial powers of the world will consider the United States of America as forming a weight in that balance of power in Europe which never can be forgotten or neglected. It would not only be against our interest, but it would be doing wrong to one-half of Europe, at least, if we should voluntarily throw ourselves into either scale. It is a natural policy for a nation that studies to be neutral to consult with other nations engaged in the same studies and pursuits. At the same time that measures might be pursued with this view, our treaties with Prussia and Sweden, one of which is expired and the other near expiring, might be renewed.

Gentlemen of the House of Representatives:

It is particularly your province to consider the state of the public finances, and to adopt such measures respecting them as exigencies shall be found to require. The preservation of public credit, the regular extinguishment of the public debt, and a provision of funds to defray any extraordinary expenses will of course call for your serious attention. Although the imposition of new burthens can not be in itself agreeable, yet there is no ground to doubt that the American people will expect from you such measures as their actual engagements, their present security, and future interests demand.

Gentlemen of the Senate and Gentlemen of the House of Representatives:

The present situation of our country imposes an obligation on all the departments of Government to adopt an explicit and decided conduct. In my situation an exposition of the principles by which my Administration will be governed ought not to be omitted.

It is impossible to conceal from ourselves or the world what has been before observed, that endeavors have been employed to foster and establish a decision between the Government and people of the United States. To investigate the causes which have encouraged this attempt is not necessary; but to repel, by decided and united councils, insinuations so derogatory to the honor and aggressions so dangerous to the Constitution, union, and even independence of the nation is an indispensable duty.

It must not be permitted to be doubted whether the people of the United States will support the Government established by their voluntary consent and appointed by their free choice, or whether, by surrendering themselves to the direction of foreign and domestic factions, in opposition to their own Government, they will forfeit the honorable station they have hitherto maintained.

For myself, having never been indifferent to what concerned the interests of my country, devoted the best part of my life to obtain and support its independence, and constantly witnessed the patriotism, fidelity, and perseverance of my fellow-citizens on the most trying occasions, it is not for me to hesitate or abandon a cause in which my heart has been so long engaged.

Convinced that the conduct of the Government has been just and impartial to foreign nations, that those internal regulations which have been established by law for the preservation of peace are in their nature proper, and that they have been fairly executed, nothing will ever be done by me to impair the national engagements, to innovate upon principles which have been so deliberately and uprightly established, or to surrender in any manner the rights of the Government. To enable me to maintain this declaration I rely, under God, with entire confidence on the firm and enlightened support of the National Legislature and upon the virtue and patriotism of my fellow-citizens.

JOHN ADAMS.

MISSION TO FRANCE
May 31, 1797

Adams' cabinet, the High Federalist secretaries, Pickering, Wolcott, and McHenry, opposed sending any mission to France, but Alexander Hamilton thought it necessary to secure public support for a defense program. Adams wanted to include a Republican, and tried to get Vice-President Thomas Jefferson to go, and failing that, to persuade James Madison to serve. The Federalist Party leaders were violently opposed to Madison and it was just as well that Madison refused.

Charles Cotesworth Pinckney, already abroad, was an obvious choice. John Marshall of Virginia, another Federalist, was satisfactory to both sides. Trouble arose in finding a moderate. Adams, as shown below, originally selected Francis Dana, who refused the appointment. Eventually Adams appointed his old friend Elbridge Gerry of Massachusetts, known as a no-party man. Gerry was finally confirmed by the Senate after a bitter debate.

UNITED STATES, May 31, 1797.

Gentlemen of the Senate:

I nominate General Charles Cotesworth Pinckney, of South Carolina, Francis Dana, chief justice of the State of Massachusetts, and General John Marshall, of Virginia, to be jointly and severally envoys extraordinary and ministers plenipotentiary to the French Republic.

After mature deliberation on the critical situation of our relations with France, which have long engaged my most serious attention, I have determined on these nominations of persons to negotiate with the French Republic to dissipate umbrages, to remove prejudices, to rectify errors, and adjust all differences by a treaty between the two powers.

It is in the present critical and singular circumstances of great importance to engage the confidence of the great portions of the Union in the characters employed and the measures which may be adopted. I have therefore thought it expedient to nominate persons of talents and integrity, long known and intrusted in the three great divisions of the Union, and at the same time, to provide against the cases of death, absence, indisposition, or other impediment, to invest any one or more of them with full powers.

JOHN ADAMS.

FIRST ANNUAL ADDRESS
November 23, 1797

Adams delivered his first annual message to Congress at a time of extreme tension. He had had word that Marshall and Gerry had arrived in Holland to join Pinckney and were proceeding to Paris. Adams stressed the importance of commerce and the need for adequate defense measures. Party differences were to become acute in this second session of the Fifth Congress, and Adams' position in his speech seemed to lean strongly to the Federalist view.

UNITED STATES, November 23, 1797.

Gentlemen of the Senate and Gentlemen of the House of Representatives:

I was for some time apprehensive that it would be necessary, on account of the contagious sickness which afflicted the city of Philadelphia, to convene the National Legislature at some other place. This measure it was desirable to avoid, because it would occasion much public inconvenience and a considerable public expense and add to the calamities of the inhabitants of this city, whose sufferings must have excited the sympathy of all their fellow-citizens. Therefore, after taking measures to ascertain the state and decline of the sickness, I postponed my determination, having hopes, now happily realized, that, without hazard to the lives or health of the members, Congress might assemble at this place, where it was next by law to meet. I submit, however, to your consideration whether a power to postpone the meeting of Congress without passing the time fixed by the Constitution upon such occasions, would not be a useful amendment to the law of 1794.

Although I can not yet congratulate you on the reestablishment of peace in Europe and the restoration of security to the persons and properties of our citizens from injustice and violence at sea, we have, nevertheless, abundant cause of gratitude to the source of benevolence and influence for interior tranquillity and personal security, for propitious seasons, prosperous agriculture, productive fisheries, and general improvements, and, above all, for a rational spirit of civil and religious liberty and a calm but steady determination to support our sovereignty, as well as our moral and our religious principles, against all open and secret attacks.

Our envoys extraordinary to the French Republic embarked—one in July, the other early in August—to join their colleague in Holland. I have received intelligence of the arrival of both of them in Holland, from whence they all proceeded on their journeys to Paris within a few days of the 19th of September. Whatever may be the result of this mission, I trust that nothing will have been omitted on my part to conduct the negotiation to a successful conclusion, on such equitable terms as may be compatible with the safety, honor, and interest of the United States. Nothing, in the meantime, will contribute so much to the preservation of peace and the attainment of justice as a manifestation of that energy and unanimity of which on many former occasions the people of the United States have given such memorable proofs, and the exertion of those resources for national defense which a beneficient Providence has kindly placed within their power.

It may be confidently asserted that nothing has occurred since the adjournment of Congress which renders inexpedient those precautionary measures recommended by me to the consideration of the two Houses at the opening of your late extraordinary session. If that system was then prudent, it is more so now, as increasing depredations strengthen the reasons for its adoption.

Indeed, whatever may be the issue of the negotiation with France, and whether the war in Europe is or is not to continue, I hold it most certain that permanent tranquillity and order will not soon be obtained. The state of society has so long been disturbed, the sense of moral and religious obligations so much weakened, public faith and national honor have been so impaired, respect to treaties has been so diminished, and the laws of nations has lost so much of its force, while pride, ambition, avarice, and violence have been so long unrestrained, there remains no reasonable ground on which to raise an expectation that a commerce without protection or defense will not be plundered.

The commerce of the United States is essential, if not to their existence, at least to their comfort, their growth, prosperity, and happiness. The genius, character, and habits of the people are highly commercial. Their cities have been formed and exist upon commerce. Our agriculture, fisheries, arts, and manufactures are connected with and depend upon it. In short, commerce has made this country what it is, and it can not be destroyed or neglected without involving the people in poverty and distress. Great numbers are directly and solely supported by navigation. The faith of society is pledged for the preservation of the rights of commercial and seafaring no less than of the other citizens. Under this view of our affairs, I should hold myself guilty of a neglect of duty if I forbore to recommend that we should make every exertion to protect our commerce and to place our country in a suitable posture of defense as the only sure means of preserving both.

I have entertained an expectation that it would have been in my power at the opening of this session to have communicated to you the agreeable information of the due execution of our treaty with His Catholic Majesty respecting the withdrawing of his troops from our territory and the demarcation of the line of limits, but by the latest authentic intelligence Spanish garrisons were still continued within our country, and the running of the boundary line had not been commenced. These circumstances are the more to be regretted as they can not fail to affect the Indians in a manner injurious to the United States. Still, however, indulging the hope that the answers which have been given will remove the objections offered by the Spanish officers to the immediate execution of the treaty, I have judged it proper that we should continue in readiness to receive the posts and to run the line of limits. Further information on this subject will be communicated in the course of the session.

In connection with this unpleasant state of things on our western frontier it is proper for me to mention the attempts of foreign agents to alienate the affections of the Indian nations and to excite them to actual hostilities against the United States. Great activity has been exerted by those persons who have insinuated themselves among the Indian tribes residing within the territory of the United States to influence them to transfer their affections and force to a foreign nation, to form them into a confederacy, and prepare them for war against the United States. Although measures have been taken to counteract these infractions of our rights, to prevent Indian hostilities, and to preserve entire their attachment to the United States, it is my duty to observe that to give a better effect to these measures and to obviate the consequences of a repetition of such practices a law providing adequate punishment for such offenses may be necessary.

The commissioners appointed under the fifth article of the treaty of amity, commerce, and navigation between the United States and Great Britain to ascertain the river which was truly intended under the name of the river St. Croix mentioned in the treaty of peace, met at Passamaquoddy Bay in October, 1796, and viewed the mouths of the rivers in question and the adjacent shores and islands, and, being of opinion that actual surveys of both rivers to their sources were necessary, gave to the agents of the two nations instructions for that purpose, and adjourned to meet at Boston in August. They met, but the surveys requiring more time than had been supposed, and not being then completed, the commissioners again adjourned, to meet at Providence, in the State of Rhode Island, in June next, when we may expect a final examination and decision.

The commissioners appointed in pursuance of the sixth article of the treaty met at Philadelphia in May last to examine the claims of British subjects for debts contracted before the peace and still remaining due to them from citizens or inhabitants of the United States. Various causes have hitherto prevented any determinations, but the business is now resumed, and doubtless will be prosecuted without interruption.

Several decisions on the claims of citizens of the United States for losses and damages sustained by reason of irregular and illegal captures or condemnations of their vessels or other property have been made by the commissioners in London conformably to the seventh article of the treaty. The sums awarded by the commissioners have been paid by the British Government. A considerable number of other claims, where costs and damages, and not captured property, were the only objects in question, have been decided by arbitration, and the sums awarded to the citizens of the United States have also been paid.

The commissioners appointed agreeably to the twenty-first article of our treaty with Spain met at Philadelphia in the summer past to examine and decide on the claims of our citizens for losses they have sustained in consequence of their vessels and cargoes having been taken by the subjects of His Catholic Majesty during the late war between Spain and France. Their sittings have been interrupted, but are now resumed.

The United States being obligated to make compensation for the losses and damages sustained by British subjects, upon the award of the commissioners acting under the sixth article of the treaty with Great Britain, and for the losses and damages sustained by British subjects by reason of the capture of their vessels and merchandise taken within the limits and jurisdiction of the United States and brought into their ports, or taken by vessels originally armed in ports of the United States, upon the awards of the commissioners acting under the seventh article of the same treaty, it is necessary that provision be made for fulfilling these obligations.

The numerous captures of American vessels by the cruisers of the French Republic and of some by those of Spain have occasioned considerable expenses in making and supporting the claims of our citizens before their tribunals. The sums required for this purpose have in divers instances been disbursed by the consuls of the United States. By means of the same captures great numbers of our seamen have been thrown ashore in foreign countries, destitute of all means of subsistence, and the sick in particular have been exposed to grievous sufferings. The consuls have in these cases also advanced moneys for their relief. For these advances they reasonably expect reimbursements from the United States.

The consular act relative to seamen requires revision and amendment. The provisions for their support in foreign countries and for their return are found to be inadequate and ineffectual. Another provision seems necessary to be added to the consular act. Some foreign vessels have been discovered sailing under the flag of the United States and with forged papers. It seldom happens that the consuls can detect this deception, because they have no authority to demand an inspection of the registers and sea letters.

Gentlemen of the House of Representatives:

It is my duty to recommend to your serious consideration those objects which by the Constitution are placed particularly within your sphere—the national debts and taxes.

Since the decay of the feudal system, by which the public defense was provided for chiefly at the expense of individuals, the system of loans has been introduced, and as no nation can raise within the year by taxes sufficient sums for its defense and military operations in time of war, the sums loaned and debts contracted have necessarily become the subjects of what have been called funding systems. The consequences arising from the continual accumulation of public debts in other countries ought to admonish us to be careful to prevent their growth in our own. The national defense must be provided for as well as the support of Government; but both should be accomplished as much as possible by immediate taxes, and as little as possible by loans.

The estimates for the service of the ensuing year will by my direction be laid before you.

Gentlemen of the Senate and Gentlemen of the House of Representatives:

We are met together at a most interesting period. The situations of the principal powers of Europe are singular and portentous. Connected with some by treaties and with all by commerce, no important event there can be indifferent to us. Such circumstances call with peculiar importunity not less for a disposition to unite in all those measures on which the honor, safety, and prosperity of our country depend than for all the exertions of wisdom and firmness.

In all such measures you may rely on my zealous and hearty concurrence.

JOHN ADAMS.

REPORT TO CONGRESS ON FAILURE OF MISSION
March 19, 1798

Adams here reported the failure of the French to receive Pinckney, Marshall, and Gerry and his removal of restrictions on arming our ships. This was tantamount to admitting a state of a war with France. Adams withheld the actual dispatches or any indication of the XYZ insult, probably to protect our ministers still in Europe.

UNITED STATES, March 19, 1798.

Gentlemen of the Senate and Gentlemen of the House of Representatives:

The dispatches from the envoys extraordinary of the United States to the French Republic, which were mentioned in my message to both Houses of Congress of the 5th instant, have been examined and maturely considered.

While I feel a satisfaction in informing you that their exertions for the adjustment of the differences between the two nations have been sincere and unremitted, it is incumbent on me to declare that I perceive no ground of expectation that the objects of their mission can be accomplished on terms compatible with the safety, the honor, or the essential interests of the nation.

This result can not with justice be attributed to any want of moderation on the part of this Government, or to any indisposition to forego secondary interests for the preservation of peace. Knowing it to be my duty, and believing it to be your wish, as well as that of the great body of the people, to avoid by all reasonable concessions any participation in the contentions of Europe, the powers vested in our envoys were commensurate with a liberal and pacific policy and that high confidence which might justly be reposed in the abilities, patriotism, and integrity of the characters to whom the negotiation was committed. After a careful review of the whole subject, with the aid of all the information I have received, I can discern nothing which could have insured or contributed to success that has been omitted on my part, and nothing further which can be attempted consistently with maxims for which our country has contended at every hazard, and which constitute the basis of our national sovereignty.

Under these circumstances I can not forbear to reiterate the recommendations which I have been formerly made, and to exhort you to adopt with promptitude, decision, and unanimity such measures as the ample resources of the country afford for the protection of our seafaring and commercial citizens, for the defense of any exposed portions of our territory, for replenishing our arsenals, establishing foundries and military manufactures, and to provide such efficient revenue as will be necessary to defray extraordinary expenses and supply the deficiencies which may be occasioned by depredations on our commerce.

The present state of things is so essentially different from that in which instructions were given to the collectors to restrain vessels of the United States from sailing in an armed condition that the principle on which those orders were issued has ceased to exist. I therefore deem it proper to inform Congress that I no longer conceive myself justifiable in continuing them, unless in particular cases where there may be reasonable ground of suspicion that such vessels are intended to be employed contrary to law.

In all your proceedings it will be important to manifest a zeal, vigor, and concert in defense of the national rights proportioned to the danger with which they are threatened.

JOHN ADAMS.

RELEASE OF THE XYZ PAPERS
April 3, 1798

Republicans launched a move to demand to see the dispatches from our mission to Europe. High Federalists joined them, and the combination carried a motion in the House of Representatives on April 2, asking President Adams to release the papers. This Adams did the next day and the resulting outrage about the treatment of our envoys backfired on the Republicans and resulted in intense anti-French and strong nationalistic feelings in both parties.

UNITED STATES, April 3, 1798.

Gentlemen of the Senate and Gentlemen of the House of Representatives:

In compliance with the request of the House of Representatives expressed in their resolution of the 2d of this month, I transmit to both Houses those instructions to and dispatches from the envoys extraordinary of the United States to the French Republic which were mentioned in my message of the 19th of March last, omitting only some names and a few expressions descriptive of the persons.

I request that they may be considered in confidence until the members of Congress are fully possessed of their contents and shall have had opportunity to deliberate on the consequences of their publication, after which time I submit them to your wisdom.

JOHN ADAMS.

NATURALIZATION ACT
June 18, 1798

This was the first of a group of laws usually known collectively as the Alien and Sedition Acts. They were a reaction to the extreme partisanship which was enveloping the country during the threat of a war with France. Since many of the leading Republican spokesmen were refugees from Europe the Federalists passed measures such as this. A Naturalization Act of January 29, 1795 had provided a residence of five years for aliens before naturalization. The new act extended the period to fourteen years and prescribed the registration of aliens. The latter provision was particularly insulting to newcomers.

In 1802, with Republicans in control, the 1795 provisions were restored.

An Act supplementary to and to amend the act, intituled "An act to establish an uniform rule of naturalization; and to repeal the act heretofore passed on that subject."

SECTION 1. **Be it enacted by the Senate and House of Representatives of the United States of America in Congress assembled,** That no alien shall be admitted to become a citizen of the United States, or of any state, unless in the manner prescribed by the act, intituled "An act to establish an uniform rule of naturalization; and to repeal the act heretofore passed on that subject," he shall have declared his intention to become a citizen of the United States, five years, at least, before his admission, and shall, at the time of his application to be admitted, declare and prove, to the satisfaction of the court having jurisdiction in the case, that he has resided within the United States fourteen years, at least, and within the state or territory where, or for which such court is at the time held, five years, at least, besides conforming to the other declarations, renunciations and proofs, by the said act required, any thing therein to the contrary hereof notwithstanding: **Provided,** that any alien, who was residing within the limits, and under the jurisdiction of the United States, before the twenty-ninth day of January, one thousand seven hundred and ninety-five, may, within one year after the passing of this act—and any alien who shall have made the declaration of his intention to become a citizen of the United States, in conformity to the provisions of the act (of Jan. 29, 1795), may, within four years after having made the declaration, aforesaid, be admitted to become a citizen, in the manner prescribed by the said act, upon his making proof that he has resided five years, at least, within the limits, and under the jurisdiction of the United States: **And provided also,** that no alien, who shall be a native, citizen, denizen or subject of any nation or state with whom the United States shall be at war, at the time of his application, shall be then admitted to become a citizen of the United States.

SEC. 2. (Abstracts of the declarations of aliens seeking naturalization to be sent to the Secretary of State by clerks of courts, under penalty for refusal.)

SEC. 3. (Certified copies of records of naturalization, including all cases before the passage of this act, to be sent to the Secretary of State by clerks of courts, under penalty for wilful neglect.)

SEC. 4. **And be it further enacted,** That all white persons, aliens, (accredited foreign ministers, consuls, or agents, their families and domestics, excepted) who, after the passing of this act, shall continue to reside, or who shall arrive, or come to reside in any port or place within the territory of the United States, shall be reported, if free, and of the age of twenty-one years, by themselves, or being under the age of twenty-one years, or holden in service, by their parent, guardian, master or mistress in whose care they shall be, to the clerk of the district court of the district, if living within ten miles of the port or place, in which their residence or arrival shall be, and otherwise, to the collector of such port or place, or some officer or other person there, or nearest thereto, who shall be authorized by the President of the United States, to register aliens: and report, as aforesaid, shall be made in all cases of residence, within six months from and after the passing of this act, and in all after cases, within forty-eight hours after the first arrival or coming into the territory of the United States, and shall ascertain the sex, place of birth, age, nation, place of allegiance or citizenship, condition or occupation, and place of actual or intended residence within the United States, of the alien or aliens reported, and by whom the report is made. (The report to be recorded, &c.) And the clerk of each district court shall, during one year from the passing of this act, make monthly returns to the department of State, of all aliens registered and returned, as aforesaid, in his office.

SEC. 5. **And be it further enacted,** That every alien who shall continue to reside, or who shall arrive, as aforesaid, of whom a report is required as aforesaid, who shall refuse or neglect to make such report, and to receive a certificate thereof, shall forfeit and pay the sum of two dollars; and any justice of the peace, or other civil magistrate, who has authority to require surety of the peace, shall and may, on complaint to him made thereof, cause such alien to be brought before him, there to give surety of the peace and good behaviour during his residence within the United States, or for such term as the justice or other magistrate shall deem reasonable, and until a report and registry of such alien shall be made, and a certificate thereof, received as aforesaid; and in failure of such surety, such alien shall and may be committed to the common gaol, and shall be there held, until the order which the justice or magistrate shall and may reasonably make, in the premises, shall be performed. And every person, whether alien, or other, having the care of any alien or aliens, under the age of twenty-one years, or of any white alien holden in service, who shall refuse and neglect to make report thereof, as aforesaid, shall forfeit the sum of two dollars, for each and every such minor or servant, monthly, and every month, until a report and registry, and a certificate thereof, shall be had, as aforesaid.

SEC. 6. **And be it further enacted,** That in respect to every alien, who shall come to reside within the United States after the passing of this act, the time of the registry of such alien shall be taken to be the time when the term of residence within the limits, and under the jurisdiction of the United States, shall have commenced, in case of an application by such alien, to be admitted a citizen of the United States; and a certificate of such registry shall be required, in proof of the term of residence, by the court to whom such application shall and may be made.

SEC. 7. **And be it further enacted,** That all and singular the penalties established by this act, shall and may be recovered in the name, and to the use of any person, who will inform and sue for the same, before any judge, justice, or court, having jurisdiction in such case, and to the amount of such penalty, respectively.

JOHN ADAMS

MESSAGE TO CONGRESS
June 21, 1798

The summer of 1798 was marked by preparations for a war with France, and for Federalist attempts to curtail any criticisms of their anti-French policies. The Alien and Sedition Laws were in preparation and soon to be adopted and an army authorized, with General Washington named as its Commander-in-Chief. Adams' message here, therefore, was marked by its restraint.

UNITED STATES, June 21, 1798.

Gentlemen of the Senate and Gentlemen of the House of Representatives:

While I congratulate you on the arrival of General Marshall, one of our late envoys extraordinary to the French Republic, at a place of safety, where he is justly held in honor, I think it my duty to communicate to you a letter received by him from Mr. Gerry, the only one of the three who has not received his conge. This letter, together with another from the minister of foreign relations to him of the 3d of April, and his answer of the 4th, will shew the situation in which he remains—his intentions and prospects.

I presume that before this time he has received fresh instructions (a copy of which accompanies this message) to consent to no loans, and therefore the negotiation may be considered at an end.

I will never send another minister to France without assurances that he will be received, respected, and honored as the representative of a great, free, powerful, and independent nation.

JOHN ADAMS.

ALIEN ACT
June 25, 1798

The President was authorized by this measure to order from the country all aliens regarded as dangerous to the peace and safety of the United States or suspected of being involved in treasonable activities. Republicans opposed the law as a grant of arbitrary power to the Chief Executive and as being directed against such learned men (but Federalist enemies) as Joseph Priestley, the celebrated English scientist.

An Act concerning Aliens.

SECTION 1. **Be it enacted by the Senate and House of Representatives of the United States of America in Congress assembled,** That it shall be lawful for the President of the United States at any time during the continuance of this act, to **order** all such **aliens as** he shall judge dangerous to the peace and safety of the United States, or shall have reasonable grounds to suspect are concerned in any treasonable or secret machinations against the government thereof, to depart out of the territory of the United States, within such time as shall be expressed in such order, which order shall be served on such alien by delivering him a copy thereof, or leaving the same at his usual abode, and returned to the office of the Secretary of State, by the marshal or other person to whom the same shall be directed. And in case any alien, so ordered to depart, shall be found at large within the United States after the time limited in such order for his departure, and not having obtained a **license** from the President to reside therein, or having obtained such **license** shall not have conformed thereto, every such alien, shall, on conviction thereof, be imprisoned for a term not exceeding three years, and shall never after be admitted to become a citizen of the United States. **Provided always, and be it further enacted,** that if any alien so ordered to depart shall prove to the satisfaction of the President, by evidence to be taken before such person or persons as the President shall direct, who are for that purpose hereby authorized to administer oaths, that no injury or danger to the United States will arise from suffering such alien to reside therein, the President may grant a **license** to such alien to remain within the United States for such time as he shall judge proper, and at such place as he may designate. And the President may also require of such alien to enter into a bond to the United States, in such penal sum as he may direct, with one or more sufficient sureties to the satisfaction of the person authorized by the President to take the same, conditioned for the good behavior of such alien during his residence in the United States, and not violating his license, which license the President may revoke, whenever he shall think proper.

SEC. 2. **And be it further enacted,** That it shall be lawful for the President of the United States, whenever he may deem it necessary for the public safety, to order to be removed out of the territory thereof, any alien who may or shall be in prison in pursuance of this act; and to cause to be arrested and sent out of the United States such of those aliens as shall have been ordered to depart therefrom and shall not have obtained a license as aforesaid, in all cases where, in the opinion of the President, the public safety requires a speedy removal. And if any alien so removed or sent out of the United States by the President shall voluntarily return thereto, unless by permission of the President of the United States, such alien on conviction thereof, shall be imprisoned so long as, in the opinion of the President, the public safety may require.

SEC. 3. **And be it further enacted,** That every master or commander of any ship or vessel which shall come into any port of the United States after the first day of July next, shall immediately on his arrival make report in writing to the collector or other chief officer of the customs of such port, of all aliens, if any, on board his vessel, specifying their names, age, the place of nativity, the country from which they shall have come, the nation to which they belong and owe allegiance, their occupation and a description of their persons, as far as he shall be informed thereof, and on failure, every such master and commander shall forfeit and pay three hundred dollars, for the payment whereof on default of such master or commander, such vessel shall also be holden, and may by such collector or other officer of the customs be detained. And it shall be the duty of such collector or other officer of the customs, forthwith to transmit to the office of the department of state true copies of all such returns.

SEC. 4. **And be it further enacted,** That the circuit and district courts of the United States, shall respectively have cognizance of all crimes and offences against this act. And all marshals and other officers of the United States are required to execute all precepts and orders of the President of the United States issued in pursuance or by virtue of this act.

SEC. 5. **And be it further enacted,** That it shall be lawful for any alien who may be ordered to be removed from the United States, by virtue of this act, to take with him such part of his goods, chattels, or other property, as he may find convenient; and all property left in the United States by any alien, who may be removed, as aforesaid, shall be, and remain subject to his order and disposal, in the same manner as if this act had not been passed.

SEC. 6. **And be it further enacted,** That this act shall continue and be in force for and during the term of two years from the passing thereof.

ALIEN ENEMIES ACT
July 6, 1798

This measure would authorize the President to remove from the country aliens who were natives or citizens of a country with whom we were in a "declared war." Since no war was declared against France it was not put into effect.

An Act respecting Alien Enemies.

SECTION 1. **Be it enacted by the Senate and House of Representatives of the United States of America in Congress assembled,** That whenever there shall be a declared war between the United States and any foreign nation or government, or any invasion or predatory incursion shall be perpetrated, attempted, or threatened against the territory of the United States, by any foreign nation or government, and the President of the United States shall make public proclamation of the event, all natives, citizens, denizens, or subjects of the hostile nation or government, being males of the age of fourteen years and upwards, who shall be within the United States, and not actually naturalized, shall be liable to be apprehended, restrained, secured and removed, as alien enemies. And the President of the United States shall be, and he is hereby authorized, in any event, as aforesaid, by his proclamation thereof, or other public act, to direct the conduct to be observed, on the part of the United States, towards the aliens who shall become liable, as aforesaid; the manner and degree of the restraint to which they shall be subject, and in what cases, and upon what security their residence shall be permitted, and to provide for the removal of those, who, not being permitted to reside within the United States, shall refuse or neglect to depart therefrom; and to establish any other regulations which shall be found necessary in the premises and for the public safety: Provided, that aliens resident within the United States, who shall become liable as enemies, in the manner aforesaid, and who shall not be chargeable with actual hostility, or other crime against the public safety, shall be allowed, for the recovery, disposal, and removal of their goods and effects, and for their departure, the full time which is, or shall be stipulated by any treaty, where any shall have been between the United States, and the hostile nation or government, of which they shall be natives, citizens, denizens or subjects: and when no such treaty shall have existed, the President of the United States may ascertain and declare such reasonable time as may be consistent with the public safety, and according to the dictates of humanity and national hospitality.

SEC. 2. **And be it further enacted,** That after any proclamation shall be made as aforesaid, it shall be the duty of the several courts of the United States, and of each state, having criminal jurisdiction, and of the several judges and justices of the courts of the United States, and they shall be, and are hereby respectively, authorized upon complaint, against any alien or alien enemies, as aforesaid, who shall be resident and at large within such jurisdiction or district, to the danger of the public peace or safety, and contrary to the tenor or intent of such proclamation, or other regulations which the President of the United States shall and may establish in the premises, to cause such alien or aliens to be duly apprehended and convened before such court, judge or justice; and after a full examination and hearing on such complaint, and sufficient cause therefor appearing, shall and may order such alien or aliens to be removed out of the territory of the United States, or to give sureties of their good behaviour, or to be otherwise restrained, conformably to the proclamation or regulations which shall or may be established as aforesaid, and may imprison, or otherwise secure such alien or aliens, until the order which shall and may be made, as aforesaid, shall be performed.

SEC. 3. **And be it further enacted,** That it shall be the duty of the marshall of the district in which any alien enemy shall be apprehended, who by the President of the United States, or by order of any court, judge or justice, as aforesaid, shall be required to depart, and to be removed, as aforesaid, to provide therefor, and to execute such order, by himself or his deputy, or other discreet person or persons to be employed by him, by causing a removal of such alien out of the territory of the United States; and for such removal the marshal shall have the warrant of the President of the United States, or of the court, judge or justice ordering the same, as the case may be.

SEDITION ACT
July 14, 1798

One of the most controversial laws in American history, the Sedition Act provided fines and imprisonment for "false, scandalous and malicious" writings or utterances against the government or its officials. The intent and enforcement of the law, particularly by Timothy Pickering, seemed political rather than being aimed at curbing sedition. Fifteen persons were indicted under the law, all Republicans, and ten were found guilty. Thomas Cooper, a friend of Joseph Priestley, was sentenced to six months imprisonment for writing some uncomplimentary, although certainly not subversive, remarks about Adams.

An Act in addition to the act, entitled "An Act for the punishment of certain crimes against the United States."

SECTION 1. **Be it enacted by the Senate and House of Representatives of the United States of America, in Congress assembled,** That if any persons shall unlawfully combine or conspire together, with intent to oppose any measure or measures of the government of the United States, which are or shall be directed by proper authority, or to impede the operation of any law of the United States, or to intimidate or prevent any person holding a place or office in or under the government of the United States, from undertaking, performing or executing his trust or duty; and if any person, or persons, with intent as aforesaid, shall counsel, advise or attempt to procure any insurrection, riot, unlawful assembly, or combination, whether such conspiracy, threatening, counsel, advice or attempt shall have the proposed effect or not, he or they shall be deemed guilty of a high misdemeanor, and on conviction, before any court of the United States having jurisdiction thereof, shall be punished by a fine not exceeding five thousand dollars, and by imprisonment during a term not less than six months nor exceeding five years; and further, at the discretion of the court may be holden to find sureties for his good behaviour in such sum, and for such time, as the said court may direct.

SEC. 2. **And be it further enacted,** That if any person shall write, print, utter or publish, or shall cause or procure to be written, printed, uttered or published, or shall knowingly and willingly assist or aid in writing, printing, uttering or publishing any false, scandalous and malicious writing or writings against the government of the United States, or either House of the Congress of the United States, or the President of the United States, with intent to defame the said government, or either house of the said Congress, or the said President, or to bring them, or either of them, into contempt or disrepute; or to excite against them, or either or any of them, the hatred of the good people of the United States, or to stir up sedition within the United States, or to excite any unlawful combinations therein, for opposing or resisting any law of the United States, or any act of the President of the United States, done in pursuance of any such law, or of the powers in him vested by the constitution of the United States, or to resist, oppose, or defeat any such law or act, or to aid, encourage or abet any hostile designs of any foreign nations against the United States, their people or government, then such person, being thereof convicted before any court of the United States having jurisdiction thereof, shall be punished by a fine not exceeding two thousand dollars, and by imprisonment not exceeding two years.

SEC. 3. **And be it further enacted and declared,** That if any person shall be prosecuted under this act, for the writing or publishing any libel aforesaid, it shall be lawful for the defendant, upon the trial of the cause, to give in evidence in his defence, the truth of the matter contained in the publication charged as a libel. And the jury who shall try the cause, shall have a right to determine the law and the fact, under the direction of the court, as in other cases.

SEC. 4. **And be it further enacted,** That this act shall continue and be in force until the third day of March, one thousand eight hundred and one, and no longer: **Provided ,** that the expiration of the act shall not prevent or defeat a prosecution and punishment of any offence against the law, during the time it shall be in force.

KENTUCKY AND VIRGINIA RESOLUTION
1798, 1799

The Republican response to the Alien and Sedition Laws was embodied in the resolutions adopted by the legislatures of Virginia in 1798 and Kentucky in 1798 and 1799. James Madison wrote the Virginia Resolutions and Thomas Jefferson the Kentucky ones, although his name was not attached to them.

While the purpose of the Resolutions was to oppose the obnoxious Alien and Sedition Acts, the concept of the compact theory of government, of nullification (voiding federal law by state action), and of states rights in general was expressed in these resolves. They were to be applied by New Englanders in 1814 (the Hartford Convention) and by South Carolinians in 1832 (Nullification) depending on the particular issue involved. In another sense the Kentucky and Virginia Resolutions were in the best tradition of the right of free speech as expressed in the First Amendment to the Constitution.

KENTUCKY LEGISLATURE.

In the House of Representatives, November 10, 1798.

The House, according to the standing order of the day, resolved itself into a Committee of the Whole on the state of the Commonwealth, Mr. Caldwell in the chair. And after some time spent therein the Speaker resumed the chair, and Mr. Caldwell reported that the Committee had, according to order, had under consideration the Governor's Address, and had come to the following Resolutions thereupon, which he delivered in at the clerk's table, where they were twice read and agreed to by the House.

I. **Resolved,** that the several States composing the United States of America, are not united on the principle of unlimited submission to their general government; but that by compact under the style and title of a Constitution for the United States and of amendments thereto, they constituted a general government for special purposes, delegated to that government certain definite powers, reserving each State to itself, the residuary mass of right to their own self-government; and that whensoever the general government assumes undelegated powers, its acts are unauthoritative, void, and of no force: That to this compact each State acceded as a State, and is an integral party, its co-States forming, as to itself, the other party: That the government created by this compact was not made the exclusive or final judge of the extent of the powers delegated to itself; since that would have made its discretion, and not the Constitution, the measure of its powers; but that as in all other cases of compact among parties having no common Judge, each party has an equal right to judge for itself, as well of infractions as of the mode and measure of redress.

II. **Resolved,** that the Constitution of the United States having delegated to Congress a power to punish treason, counterfeiting the securities and current coin of the United States, piracies and felonies committed on the high seas, and offenses against the laws of nations, and no other crimes whatever, and it being true as a general principle, and one of the amendments to the Constitution having also declared "that the powers not delegated to the United States by the Constitution, nor prohibited by it to the States, are reserved to the States respectively, or to the people," therefore also the same act of Congress passed on the 14th day of July, 1798, and entitled "An act in addition to the act entitled an act for the punishment of certain crimes against the United States;" as also the act passed by them on the 27th day of June, 1798, entitled "An act to punish frauds committed on the Bank of the United States" (and all other their acts which assume to create, define, or punish crimes other than those enumerated in the Constitution), are altogether void and of no force, and that the power to create, define, and punish such other crimes is reserved, and of right appertains solely and exclusively to the respective States, each within its own Territory.

III. **Resolved,** that it is true as a general principle, and is also expressly declared by one of the amendments to the Constitution that "the powers not delegated to the United States by the Constitution, nor prohibited by it to the States, are reserved to the States respectively or to the people;" and that no power over the freedom of religion, freedom of speech, or freedom of the press being delegated to the United States by the Constitution, nor prohibited by it to the States, all lawful powers respecting the same did of right remain, and were reserved to the States, or to the people: That thus was manifested their determination to retain to themselves the right of judging how far the licentiousness of speech and of the press may be abridged without lessening their useful freedom, and how far those abuses which cannot be separated from their use should be tolerated rather than the use be destroyed; and thus also they guarded against all abridgement by the United States of the freedom of religious opinions and exercises, and retained to themselves the right of protecting the same, as this State, by a law passed on the general demand of its citizens, had already protected them from all human restraint or interference: And that in addition to this general principle and express declaration, another and more special provision has been made by one of the amendments to the Constitution which expressly declares, that "Congress shall make no law respecting an establishment of religion, or prohibiting the free exercise thereof, or abriding the freedom of speech, or of the press." thereby guarding in the same sentence, and under the same words, the freedom of religion, of speech, and of the press, insomuch, that whatever violates either, throws down the sanctuary which covers the others, and that libels, falsehoods, defamation equally with heresy and false religion, are withheld from the cognizance of Federal tribunals. That therefore the act of the Congress of the United States passed on the 14th day of July, 1798, entitled "An act in addition to the act for the punishment of certain crimes against the United States," which does abridge the freedom of the press, is not law, but is altogether void and of no effect.

IV. **Resolved,** that alien friends are under the jurisdiction and protection of the laws of the State wherein they are; that no power over them has been delegated to the United States, nor prohibited to the individual States distinct from their power over citizens; and it being true as a general principle, and one of the amendments to the Constitution having also declared that "the powers not delegated to the United States by the Constitution, nor prohibited by it to the States, are reserved to the States respectively, or to the people," the act of the Congress of the United States passed on the 22d day of June, 1798, entitled "An act concerning aliens," which assumes power over alien friends not delegated by the Constitution, is not law, but is altogether void and of no force.

V. **Resolved,** that in addition to the general principle as well as the express declaration, that powers not delegated are reserved, another and more special provision inserted in the Constitution from abundant caution has declared, "that the migration or importation of such persons as any of the States now existing shall think proper to admit, shall not be prohibited by the Congress prior to the year 1808." That this Commonwealth does admit the migration of alien friends described as the subject of the said act concerning aliens; that a provision against prohibiting their migration is a provision against all acts equivalent thereto, or it would be nugatory; that to remove them when migrated is equivalent to a prohibition of their migration, and is therefore contrary to the said provision of the Constitution, and void.

VI. **Resolved,** that the imprisonment of a person under the protection of the laws of this Commonwealth on his failure to obey the simple order of the President to depart out of the United States, as is undertaken by the said act entitled "An act concerning aliens," is contrary to the Constitution, one amendment to which has provided, that "no person shall be deprived of liberty without the due process of law," and that another having provided "that in all criminal prosecutions, the accused shall enjoy the right to a public trial by an impartial jury, to be informed of the nature and cause of the accusation, to be confronted with the witnesses against him, to have compulsory process for obtaining witnesses in his favour, and to have the assistance of counsel for his defense," the same act undertaking to authorize the President to remove a person out of the United States, who is under the protection of the law, on his own suspicion, without accusation, without jury, without public trial, without confrontation of the witnesses against him, without having witnesses in his favour, without defense, without counsel, is contrary to these provisions also of the Constitution, is therefore not law, but utterly void and of no force. That transferring the power of judging any person who is under the protection of the laws, from the courts to the President of the United States, as is undertaken by the same act concerning aliens, is against the article of the Constitution which provides, that "the judicial power of the United States shall be vested in courts, the judges of which .shall hold their offices during good behavior," and that the said act is void for that reason also; and it is further to be noted, that this transfer of judiciary power is to that magistrate of the general government who already possesses all the executive, and a qualified negative in all the legislative powers.

VII. **Resolved,** that the construction applied by the general government (as is evinced by sundry of their proceedings) to those parts of the Constitution of the United States which delegate to Congress a power to lay and collect taxes, duties, imposts, and excises; to pay the debts, and provide for the common defense, and general welfare of the United States, and to make all laws which shall be necessary and proper for carrying into execution the powers vested by the Constitution in the government of the United States, or any department thereof, goes to the destruction of all the limits prescribed to their power by the Constitution: That words meant by that instrument to be subsiduary only to the execution of the limited powers ought not to be so construed as themselves to give unlimited powers, nor a part so to be taken as to destroy the whole residue of the instrument: That the proceedings of the general government under color of these articles will be a fit and necessary subject for revisal and correction at a time of greater tranquillity, while those specified in the preceding resolutions call for immediate redress.

VIII. **Resolved,** that the preceding Resolutions be transmitted to the Senators and Representatives in Congress from this Commonwealth, who are hereby enjoined to present the same to their respective Houses, and to use their best endeavors to procure, at the next session of Congress, a repeal of the aforesaid unconstitutional and obnoxious acts.

IX. **Resolved,** lastly, that the Governor of this Commonwealth be, and is hereby authorized and requested to communicate the preceding Resolutions to the Legislatures of the several States, to assure them that this Commonwealth considers Union for specified National purposes, and particularly for those specified in their late Federal Compact, to be friendly to the peace, happiness, and prosperity of all the States: that faithful to that compact according to the plain intent and meaning in which it was understood and acceded to by the several parties, it is sincerely anxious for its preservation: that it does also believe, that to take from the States all the powers of self-government, and transfer them to a general and consolidated government, without regard to the special delegations and reservations solemnly agreed to in that compact, is not for the peace, happiness, or properity of these States: And that, therefore, this Commonwealth is determined, as it doubts not its co-States are, tamely to submit to undelegated and consequently unlimited powers in no man or body of men on earth: that if the acts before specified should stand, these conclusions would flow from them; that the general government may place any act they think proper on the list of crimes and punish it themselves, whether enumerated or not enumerated by the Constitution as cognizable by them: that they may transfer its cognizance to the President or any other person, whose may himself be the accuser, counsel, judge, and jury, whose suspicions may be the evidence, his order the sentence, his officer the executioner, and his breast the sole record of the transaction. that a very numerous and valuable description of the inhabitants of these States being by this precedent reduced as outlaws to the absolute dominion of one man, and the barrier of the Constitution thus swept away from us all, no rampart now remains against the passions and the powers of a majority of Congress, to protect from a like exportation or other more grievous punishment the minority of the same body, the legislatures, judges, governors, and counselors of the States, nor their other peaceable inhabitants who may venture to reclaim the constitutional rights and liberties of the State and people, or who for other causes, good or bad, may be obnoxious to the views or marked by the suspicions of the President, or be thought dangerous to his or their elections or other interests, public or personal: that the friendless alien has indeed been selected as the safest subject of a first experiment, but the citizen will soon follow, or rather has already followed: for, already has a sedition act marked him as its prey: that these and successive acts of the same character, unless arrested on the threshold, may tend to drive these States into revolution and blood, and will furnish new calumnies against Republican governments, and new pretexts for those who wish it to be believed, that man cannot be governed but by a rod of iron: that it would be a dangerous delusion were a confidence in the men of our choice to silence our fears for the safety of our rights: that confidence is everywhere the parent of despotism: free government is founded in jealousy and not in confidence; it is jealousy and not confidence which prescribes limited Constitutions to bind down those whom we are obliged to trust with power: that our Constitution has accordingly fixed the limits to which and no further our confidence may go; and let the honest advocate of confidence read the alien and sedition acts, and say if the Constitution has not been wise in fixing limits to the government it created, and whether we should be wise in destroyed those limits; let him say what the government is if it be not a tyranny, which the men of our choice have conferred on the President, and the President of our choice has assented to and accepted over the friendly strangers, to whom the mild spirit of our country and its laws had pledged hospitality and protection: that the men of our choice have more respected the bare suspicions of the President than the solid rights of innocence, the claims of justification, the sacred force of truth, and the forms and substance of law and justice.

In questions of power then let no more be heard of confidence in man, but bind him down from mischief by the claims of the Constitution. That this Commonwealth does therefore call on its co-States for an expression of their sentiments on the acts concerning aliens, and for the punishment of certain crimes herein before specified, plainly declaring whether these acts are or are not authorized by the Federal Compact. And it doubts not that their sense will be so announced as to prove their attachment unaltered to limited government, whether general or particular, and that the rights and liberties of their co-States will be exposed to no dangers by remaining embarked on a common bottom with their own: That they will concur with this Commonwealth in considering the said acts so palpably against the Constitution as to amount to an undisguised declaration, that the compact is not meant to be the measure of the powers of the general government, but that it will proceed in the exercise over these States of all powers whatsoever: That they will view this as seizing the rights of the States and consolidating them in the hands of the general government with a power assumed to bind the States (not merely in cases made Federal) but in all cases whatsoever, by laws made, not with their consent, but by others against their consent: That this would be to surrender the form of government we have chosen, and to live under one deriving its powers from its own will, and not from our authority; and that the co-States, recurring to their natural right in cases not made Federal, will concur in declaring these acts void and of no force, and will each unite with this Commonwealth in requesting their repeal at the next session of Congress.

VIRGINIA RESOLUTIONS

In the House of Delegates, Friday, December 21, 1798

Resolved, That the General Assembly of Virginia doth unequivocally express a firm resolution to maintain and defend the Constitution of the United States, and the Constitution of this State, against every aggression either foreign or domestic; and that they will support the Government of the United States in all measures warranted by the former.

That this Assembly most solemnly declares a warm attachment to the Union of the States, to maintain which it pledges all its powers; and that, for this end, it is their duty to watch over and oppose every infraction of those principles which constitute the only basis of that Union, because a faithful observance of them can alone secure its existence and the public happiness.

That this Assembly doth explicitly and peremptorily declare that it views the powers of the Federal Government as resulting from the compact to which the States are parties, as limited by the plain sense and intention of the instrument constituting that compact; as no further valid than they are authorized by the grants enumerated in that compact; and that, in case of a deliberate, palpable, and dangerous exercise of other powers not granted by the said compact, the States, who are parties thereto, have the right and are in duty bound to interpose for arresting thé progress of the evil, and for maintaining within their respective limits the authorities, rights, and liberties appertaining to them.

That the General Assembly doth also express its deep regret, that a spirit has in sundry instances been manifested by the Federal Government to enlarge its powers by forced constructions of the constitutional charter which defines them; and that indications have appeared of a design to expound certain general phrases (which, having been copied from the very limited grant of powers in the former Articles of Confederation, were the less liable to be misconstrued) so as to destroy the meaning and effect of the particular enumeration which necessarily explains and limits the general phrases; and so as to consolidate the States, by degrees, into one sovereignty, the obvious tendency and inevitable consequence of which would be to transform the present republican system of the United States into an absolute, or, at best, a mixed monarchy.

That the General Assembly doth particularly protest against the palpable and alarming infractions of the Constitution in the two late cases of the "Alien and Sedition Acts," passed at the last session of Congress; the first of which exercises a power nowhere delegated to the Federal Government, and which, by uniting legislative and judicial powers to those of (the) executive, subvert the general principles of free government, as well as the particular organization and positive provisions of the Federal Constitution: and the other of which acts exercises, in like manner, a power not delegated by the Constitution, but, on the contrary, expressly and positively forbidden by one of the amendments thereto,—a power which, more than any other, ought to produce universal alarm, because it is levelled against the right of freely examining public characters and measures, and of free communication among the people thereon, which has ever been justly deemed the only effectual guardian of every other right.

That this State having by its Convention which ratified the Federal Constitution expressly declared that, among other essential rights, "the liberty of conscience and of the press cannot be cancelled, abridged, restrained, or modified by any authority of the United States," and from its extreme anxiety to guard these rights from every possible attack of sophistry or ambition, having, with other States, recommended an amendment for that purpose, which amendment was in due time annexed to the Constitution,—it would mark a reproachful inconsistency and criminal degeneracy, if an indifference were now shown to the palpable violation of one of the rights thus declared and secured, and to the establishment of a precedent which may be fatal to the other.

That the good people of this Commonwealth, having ever felt and continuing to feel the most sincere affection for their brethren of the other States, the truest anxiety for establishing and perpetuating the union of all and the most scrupulous fidelity to that Constitution, which is the pledge of mutual friendship, and the instrument of mutual happiness, the General Assembly doth solemnly appeal to the like dispositions of the other States, in confidence that they will concur with this Commonwealth in declaring, as it does hereby declare, that the acts aforesaid are unconstitutional; and that the necessary and proper measures will be taken by each for co-operating with this State, in maintaining unimpaired the authorities, rights, and liberties reserved to the States respectively, or to the people.

That the Governor be desired to transmit a copy of the foregoing resolutions to the Executive authority of each of the other States, with a request that the same may be communicated to the Legislature thereof; and that a copy be furnished to each of the Senators and Representatives representing this State in the Congress of the United States.

KENTUCKY RESOLUTIONS
House of Representatives, Thursday, Nov. 14th, 1799.

The House, according to the standing order of the day, resolved that into a Committee of the Whole House, on the state of the Commonwealth, Mr. Desha in the Chair; and, after some time spent therein, the speaker resumed the Chair, and Mr. Desha reported, that the Committee had taken under consideration sundry resolutions passed by several State Legislatures, on the subject of the Alien and Sedition Laws, and had come to a resolution thereupon, which he delivered in at the Clerk's table, where it was read an (and) **unanimously** agreed to by the House, as follows:

The representatives of the good people of this Commonwealth, in General Assembly convened, having maturely considered the answers of sundry States in the Union, to their resolutions passed the last session, respecting certain unconstitutional laws of Congress, commonly called the Alien and Sedition Laws, would be faithless, indeed, to themselves and to those they represent, were they silently to acquiesce in the principles and doctrines attempted to be maintained in all those answers, that of Virginia only excepted. To again enter the field of argument, and attempt more fully or forcibly to expose the unconstitutionality of those obnoxious laws, would, it is apprehended, be as unnecessary as unavailing. We cannot, however, but lament, that, in the discussion of those interesting subjects, by sundry of the Legislatures of our sister States, unfounded suggestions, and uncandid insinuations, derogatory to the true character and principles of this Commonwealth has been substituted in place of fair reasoning and sound argument. Our opinions of these alarming measures of the General Government, together with our reasons for those opinions, were detailed with decency, and with temper, and submitted to the discussion and judgment of our fellow-citizens throughout the Union. Whether the like decency and temper have been observed in the answers of most of those States, who have denied or attempted to obviate the great truths contained in those resolutions, we have now only to submit to a candid world. Faithful to the true principles of the federal Union, unconscious of any designs to disturb the harmony of that Union, and anxious only to escape the fangs of despotism, the good people of this Commonwealth are regardless of censure or calumniation. Least (Lest), however, the silence of this Commonwealth should be construed into an acquiescence in the doctrines and principles advanced and attempted to be maintained by the said answers, or at least those of our fellow-citizens throughout the Union who so widely differ from us on those important subjects, should be deluded by the expectation, that we shall be deterred from what we conceive our duty, or shrink from the principles contained in those resolutions—therefore,

Resolved, That this Commonwealth considers the Federal Union, upon the terms and for the purposes specified in the late compact, conducive to the liberty and happiness of the several States: That it does now unequivocally declare its attachment to the Union, and to that compact, agreeably to its obvious and real intention, and will be among the last to seek its dissolution: That if those who administer the General Government be permitted to transgress the limits fixed by that compact, by a total disregard to the special delegations of power therein contained, an annihilation of the State Governments, and the creation upon their ruins of a General Consolidated Government, will be the inevitable consequence: That the principle and construction contended for by sundry of the state legislatures, that the General Government is the exclusive judge of the extent of the powers delegated to it, stop nothing (short) of despotism— since the discretion of those who administer the government, and not the **Constitution,** would be the measure of their powers: That the several states who formed that instrument being sovereign and independent, have the unquestionable right to judge of the infraction; and, **That a Nullification by those sovereignties, of all unauthorized acts done under color of that instrument is the rightful remedy:** That this Commonwealth does, under the most deliberate reconsideration, declare, that the said Alien and Sedition Laws are, in their opinion, palpable violations of the said Constitution; and, however cheerfully it may be disposed to surrender its opinion to a majority of its sister states, in matters of ordinary or doubtful policy, yet, in no **(omit)** momentous regulations like the present, which so vitally wound the best rights of the citizen, it would consider a silent acquiescence as highly criminal: That although this Commonwealth, as a party to the federal compact, will bow to the laws of the Union, yet, it does, at the same (time) declare, that it will not now, or ever hereafter, cease to oppose in a constitutional manner, every attempt at what quarter soever offered, to violate that compact. And, finally, in order that no pretext or arguments may be drawn from a supposed acquiescence, on the part of this Commonwealth in the constitutionality of those laws, and be thereby used as precedents for similar future violations of the Federal compact—this Commonwealth does now enter against them its solemn PROTEST.

SECOND ANNUAL ADDRESS
December 8, 1798

At the opening of the third session of Congress Adams was being pressured by his cabinet to refrain from sending a new mission to France. Adams claimed later that they were anxious for a declaration of war, but there is no other evidence that any except Mc-Henry favored such a step. But to avoid peaceful overtures might accomplish the same purpose for the High Federalists.

Adams, however, in this speech took a more conciliatory position. He was receiving indications from the French that they would welcome a mission and he seemed to suggest we might, if assured of a respectful reception. In the meantime he advocated continued defense preparation with especial emphasis on the navy.

UNITED STATES, December 8, 1798.

Gentlemen of the Senate and Gentlemen of the House of Representatives:

While with reverence and resignation we contemplate the dispensations of Divine Providence in the alarming and destructive pestilence with which several of our cities and towns have been visited, there is cause for gratitude and mutual congratulations that the malady has disappeared and that we are again permitted to assemble in safety at the seat of Government for the discharge of our important duties. But when we reflect that this fatal disorder has within a few years made repeated ravages in some of our principal seaports, and with increased malignancy, and when we consider the magnitude of the evils arising from the interruption of public and private business, whereby the national interests are deeply affected, I think it my duty to invite the Legislature of the Union to examine the expediency of establishing suitable regulations in aid of the health laws of the respective States; for these being formed on the idea that contagious sickness may be communicated through the channels of commerce, there seems to be a necessity that Congress, who alone can regulate trade, should frame a system which, while it may tend to preserve the general health, may be compatible with the interests of commerce and the safety of the revenue.

While we think on this calamity and sympathize with the immediate sufferers, we have abundant reason to present to the Supreme Being our annual oblations of gratitude for a liberal participation in the ordinary blessings of His providence. To the usual subjects of gratitude I can not omit to add one of the first importance to our well-being and safety; I mean that spirit which has arisen in our country against the menaces and aggression of a foreign nation. A manly sense of national honor, dignity, and independence has appeared which, if encouraged and invigorated by every branch of the Government, will enable us to view undismayed the enterprises of any foreign power and become the sure foundation of national prosperity and glory.

The course of the transactions in relation to the United States and France which have come to my knowledge during your recess will be made the subject of a future communication. That communication will confirm the ultimate failure of the measures which have been taken by the Government of the United States toward an amicable adjustment of differences with that power. You will at the same time perceive that the French Government appears solicitious to impress the opinion that it is averse to a rupture with this country, and that it has in a qualified manner declared itself willing to receive a minister from the United States for the purpose of restoring a good understanding. It is unfortunate for professions of this kind that they should be expressed in terms which may countenance the inadmissible pretension of a right to prescribe the qualifications which a minister from the United States should possess, and that while France is asserting the existence of a disposition on her part to conciliate with sincerity the differences which have arisen, the sincerity of a like disposition on the part of the United States, of which so many demonstrative proofs have been given, should even be indirectly questioned. It is also worthy of observation that the decree of the Directory alleged to be intended to restrain the depredations of French cruisers on our commerce has not given, and can not give, any relief. It enjoins them to conform to all the laws of France relative to· cruising· and prizes, while these laws are themselves the sources of the depredations of which we have so long, so justly, and so fruitlessly complained.

The law of France enacted in January last, which subjects to capture and condemnation neutral vessels and their cargoes if any portion of the latter are of British fabric or produce, although the entire property belong to neutrals, instead of being rescinded has lately received a confirmation by the failure of a proposition for its repeal. While this law which is an unequivocal act of war on the commerce of the nations it attacks, continues in force those nations can see in the French Government only a power regardless of their essential rights, of their independence and sovereignty; and if they possess the means they can reconcile nothing with their interest and honor but a firm resistance.

Hitherto, therefore, nothing is discoverable in the conduct of France which ought to change or relax our measures of defense. On the contrary, to extend and invigorate them is our true policy. We have no reason to regret that these measures have been thus far adopted and pursued, and in proportion as we enlarge our view of the portentous and incalculable situation of Europe we shall discover new and cogent motives for the full development of our energies and resources.

But in demonstrating by our conduct that we do not fear war in the necessary protection of our rights and honor we shall give no room to infer that we abandon the desire of peace. An efficient preparation for war can alone insure peace. It is peace that we have uniformly and perseveringly cultivated, and harmony between us and France may be restored at her option. But to send another minister without more determinate assurances that he would be received would be an act of humiliation to which the United States ought not to submit. It must therefore be left with France (if she is indeed desirous of accommodation) to take the requisite steps. The United States will steadily observe the maxims by which they have hitherto been governed. They will respect the sacred rights of embassy; and with a sincere disposition on the part of France to desist from hostility, to make reparation for the injuries heretofore inflicted on our commerce, and to do justice in future, there will be no obstacle to the restoration of a friendly intercourse. In making to you this declaration I give a pledge to France and the world that the Executive authority of this country still adheres to the humane and pacific policy which has invariably governed its proceedings, in conformity with the wishes of the other branches of the Government and of the people of the United States. But considering the late manifestations of her policy toward foreign nations, I deem it a duty deliberately and solemnly to declare my opinion that whether we negotiate with her or not, vigorous preparations for war will be alike indispensable. These alone will give to us an equal treaty and insure its observance.

Among the measures of preparation which appear expedient, I take the liberty to recall your attention to the naval establishment. The beneficial effects of the small naval armament provided under the acts of the last session are known and acknowledged. Perhaps no country ever experienced more sudden and remarkable advantages from any measure of policy than we have derived from the arming for our maritime protection and defense. We ought without loss of time to lay the foundation for an increase of our Navy to a size sufficient to guard our coast and protect our trade. Such a naval force as it is doubtless in the power of the United States to create and maintain would also afford to them the best means of general defense by facilitating the safe transportation of troops and stores to every part of our extensive coast. To accomplish this important object, a prudent foresight requires that systematical measures be adopted for procuring at all times the requisite timber and other supplies. In what manner this shall be done I leave to your consideration.

I will now advert, gentlemen, to some matters of less moment, but proper to be communicated to the National Legislation.

After the Spanish garrisons had evacuated the posts they occupied at the Natchez and Walnut Hills the commissioner of the United States commenced his observations to ascertain the point near the Mississippi which terminated the northernmost part of the thirty-first degree of north latitude. From thence he proceeded to run the boundary line between the United States and Spain. He was afterwards joined by the Spanish commissioner, when the work of the former was confirmed, and they proceeded together to the demarcation of the line. Recent information renders it probable that the Southern Indians, either instigated to oppose the demarcation or jealous of the consequences of suffering white people to run a line over lands to which the Indian title had not been extinguished, have ere this time stopped the progress of the commissioners; and considering the mischiefs which may result from continuing the demarcation in opposition to the will of the Indian tribes, the great expense attending it, and that the boundaries which the commissioners have actually established probably extend at least as far as the Indian title has been extinguished, it will perhaps become expedient and necessary to suspend further proceedings by recalling our commissioner.

The commissioners appointed in pursuance of the fifth article of the treaty of amity, commerce, and navigation between the United States and His Britannic Majesty to determine what river was truly intended under the name of the river St. Croix mentioned in the treaty of peace, and forming a part of the boundary therein described, have finally decided that question. On the 25th of October they made their declaration that a river called Scoodiac, which falls into Passamaquoddy Bay at its northwestern quarters, was the true St. Croix intended in the treaty of peace, as far as its great fork, where one of its streams comes from the westward and the other from the northward, and that the latter stream is the continuation of the St. Croix to its source. This decision, it is understood, will preclude all contention among individual claimants, as it seems that the Scoodiac and its northern branch bound the grants of land which have been made by the respective adjoining Governments. A subordinate question, however, it has been suggested, still remains to be determined. Between the mouth of the St. Croix as now settled and what is usually called the Bay of Fundy lie a number of valuable islands. The commissioners have not continued the boundary line through any channel of these islands, and unless the bay of Passamaquoddy be a part of the Bay of Fundy this further adjustment of boundary will be necessary. But it is apprehended that this will not be a matter of any difficulty.

Such progress has been made in the examination and decision of cases of captures and condemnations of American vessels which were the subject of the seventh article of the treaty of amity, commerce, and navigation between the United States and Great Britain that it is supposed the commissioners will be able to bring their business to a conclusion in August of the ensuing year.

The commissioners acting under the twenty-fifth article of the treaty between the United States and Spain have adjusted most of the claims of our citizens for losses sustained in consequence of their vessels and cargoes having been taken by the subjects of His Catholic Majesty during the late war between France and Spain.

Various circumstances have concurred to delay the execution of the law for augmenting the military establishment, among these the desire of obtaining the fullest information to direct the best selection of officers. As this object will now be speedily accomplished, it is expected that the raising and organizing of the troops will proceed without obstacle and with effect.

Gentlemen of the House of Representatives:

I have directed an estimate of the appropriations which will be necessary for the service of the ensuing year to be laid before you, accompanied with a view of the public receipts and expenditures to a recent period. It will afford you satisfaction to infer the great extent and solidity of the public resources from the prosperous state of the finances, notwithstanding the unexampled embarrassments which have attended commerce. When you reflect on the conspicuous examples of patriotism and liberality which have been exhibited by our mercantile fellow-citizens, and how great a proportion of the public resources depends on their enterprise, you will naturally consider whether their convenience can not be promoted and reconciled with the security of the revenue by a revision of the system by which the collection is at present regulated.

During your recess measures have been steadily pursued for effecting the valuations and returns directed by the act of the last session, preliminary to the assessment and collection of a direct tax. No other delays or obstacles have been experienced except such as were expected to arise from the great extent of our country and the magnitude and novelty of the operation, and enough has been accomplished to assure a fulfillment of the views of the Legislature.

Gentlemen of the Senate and Gentlemen of the House of Representatives:

I can not close this address without once more adverting to our political situation and inculcating the essential importance of uniting in the maintenance of our dearest interests; and I trust that by the temper and wisdom of your proceedings and by a harmony of measures we shall secure to our country that weight and respect to which it is so justly entitled.

JOHN ADAMS.

THIRD ANNUAL ADDRESS
December 3, 1799

*While the Sixth Congress opened with a Federalist
majority, the party was split between the extremists and
the moderates. Adams had cut much of the ground from
under the High Federalists by sending the mission to
France over their objections. Thus, when in this message he urged peace and suggested the possibility of
retrenchments in spending, he was departing still
further from the views of the extreme faction of his
party.*

UNITED STATES, December 3, 1799.

Gentlemen of the Senate and Gentlemen of the House of Representatives:

It is with peculiar satisfaction that I meet the Sixth Congress of the
United States of America. Coming from all parts of the Union at this
critical and interesting period, the members must be fully possessed of
the sentiments and wishes of our constituents.

The flattering prospects of abundance from the labors of the people by
land and by sea; the prosperity of our extended commerce, notwithstanding interruptions occasioned by the belligerent state of a great part of the
world; the return of health, industry, and trade to those cities which
have lately been afflicted with disease, and the various and inestimable
advantages, civil and religious, which, secured under our happy frame
of government, are continued to us unimpaired, demand of the whole
American people sincere thanks to a benevolent Deity for the merciful
dispensations of His providence.

But while these numerous blessings are recollected, it is a painful duty
to advert to the ungrateful return which has been made for them by some
of the people in certain counties of Pennsylvania, where, seduced by the
arts and misrepresentations of designing men, they have openly resisted
the law directing the valuation of houses and lands. Such defiance was
given to the civil authority as rendered hopeless all further attempts
by judicial process to enforce the execution of the law, and it became
necessary to direct a military force to be employed, consisting of some
companies of regular troops, volunteers, and militia, by whose zeal and
activity, in cooperation with the judicial power, order and submission
were restored and many of the offenders arrested. Of these, some have
been convicted of misdeameanors, and others, charged with various
crimes, remain to be tried.

To give due effect to the civil administration of Government and to
insure a just execution of the laws, a revision and amendment of the
judiciary system is indispensable necessary. In this extensive country it can

not but happen that numerous questions respecting the interpretation of the laws and the rights and duties of officers and citizens must arise. On the one hand, the laws should be executed; on the other, individuals should be guarded from oppression. Neither of these objects is sufficiently assured under the present organization of the judicial department. I therefore earnestly recommend the subject to your serious consideration.

Persevering in the pacific and humane policy which had been invariably professed and sincerely pursued by the Executive authority of the United States, when indications were made on the part of the French Republic of a disposition to accommodate the existing differences between the two countries, I felt it to be my duty to prepare for meeting their advances by a nomination of ministers upon certain conditions which the honor of our country dictated, and which its moderation had given it a right to prescribe. The assurances which were required of the French Government previous to the departure of our envoys have been given through their minister of foreign relations, and I have directed them to proceed on their mission to Paris. They have full power to conclude a treaty, subject to the constitutional advice and consent of the Senate. The characters of these gentlemen are sure pledges to their country that nothing incompatible with its honor or interest, nothing inconsistent with our obligations of good faith or friendship to any other nation, will be stipulated.

It appearing probable from the information I received that our commercial intercourse with some ports in the island of St. Domingo might safely be renewed, I took such steps as seemed to be expedient to ascertain that point. The result being satisfactory, I then, in conformity with the act of Congress on the subject, directed the restraints and prohibitions of that intercourse to be discontinued on terms which were made known by proclamation. Since the renewal of this intercourse our citizens trading to those ports, with their property, have been duly respected, and privateering from those ports has ceased.

In examining the claims of British subjects by the commissioners at Philadelphia, acting under the sixth article of the treaty of amity, commerce, and navigation with Great Britain, a difference of opinion on points deemed essential in the interpretation of that article has arisen between the commissioners appointed by the United States and the other members of that board, from which the former have thought it their duty to withdraw. It is sincerely to be regretted that the execution of an article produced by a mutual spirit of amity and justice should have been thus unavoidably interrupted. It is, however, confidently expected that the same spirit of amity and the same sense of justice in which it originated will lead to satisfactory explanations. In consequence of the obstacles to the progress of the commission in Philadelphia, His Britannic Majesty has directed the commissioners appointed by him under the seventh article of the treaty relating to the British captures of American vessels to withdraw from the board sitting in London, but with the express declaration of his determination to fulfill with punctuality and good faith the engagements which His Majesty has contracted by his treaty with the United States, and that they will be instructed to resume their functions whenever the obstacles which impede the progress of the commission at Philadelphia shall be removed. It being in like manner my sincere determination, so far as the same depends on me, that with equal punctuality and good faith the engagements contracted by the United States in their treaties with His Britannic Majesty shall be fulfilled, I shall immediately instruct our minister at London to endeavor to obtain the explanations necessary to a just performance of those engagements on the part of the United States. With such dispositions on both sides, I can not entertain a doubt that all difficulties will soon be removed and that the two boards will then proceed and bring the business committed to them respectively to a satisfactory conclusion.

The act of Congress relative to the seat of the Government of the United States requiring that on the first Monday of December next it should be transferred from Philadelphia to the District chosen for its permanent seat, it is proper for me to inform you that the commissioners appointed to provide suitable buildings for the accommodation of Congress and of the President and of the public offices of the Government have made a report of the state of the buildings designed for those purposes in the city of Washington, from which they conclude that the removal of the seat of Government to that place at the time required will be practicable and the accommodation satisfactory. Their report will be laid before you.

Gentlemen of the House of Representatives:

I shall direct the estimates of the appropriations necessary for the service of the ensuing year, together with an account of the revenue and expenditure, to be laid before you. During a period in which a great portion of the civilized world has been involved in a war unusually calamitous and destructive, it was not to be expected that the United States could be exempted from extraordinary burthens. Although the period is not arrived when the measures adopted to secure our country against foreign attacks can be renounced, yet it is alike necessary for the honor of the Government and the satisfaction of the community that an exact economy should be maintained. I invite you, gentlemen, to investigate the different branches of the public expenditure. The examination will lead to beneficial retrenchments or produce a conviction of the wisdom of the measures to which the expenditure relates.

Gentlemen of the Senate and Gentlemen of the House of Representatives:

At a period like the present, when momentous changes are occurring and every hour is preparing new and great events in the political world, when a spirit of war is prevalent in almost every nation with whose affairs the interests of the United States have any connection, unsafe and precarious would be our situation were we to neglect the means of maintaining our just rights. The result of the mission to France is uncertain; but however it may terminate, a steady perseverance in a system of national defense commensurate with our resources and the situation of our country is an obvious dictate of wisdom; for, remotely as we are placed from the belligerent nations, and desirous as we are, by doing justice to all, to avoid offense to any, nothing short of the power of repelling aggressions will secure to our country a rational prospect of escaping the calamities of war or national degradation. As to myself, it is my anxious desire so to execute the trust reposed in me as to render the people of the United States prosperous and happy. I rely with entire confidence on your cooperation in objects equally your care, and that our mutual labors will serve to increase and confirm union among our fellow-citizens and an unshaken attachment to our Government.

JOHN ADAMS.

FOURTH ANNUAL ADDRESS
November 22, 1800

*A tone of quiet confidence in Adams' last message to
Congress seems to have been justified. He had avoided
war with France, the army could be disbanded, his
enemies in his party and even in his cabinet had been
discredited. Yet he was soon to learn, on December 3,
that he had been defeated for reelection.*

UNITED STATES, November 22, 1800.

Gentlemen of the Senate and Gentlemen of the House of Representatives:

Immediately after the adjournment of Congress at their last session
in Philadelphia I gave directions, in compliance with the laws, for the
removal of the public offices, records, and property. These directions
have been executed, and the public officers have since resided and con-
ducted the ordinary business of the Government in this place.

I congratulate the people of the United States on the assembling of
Congress at the permanent seat of their Government, and I congratulate you, gentlemen, on the prospect of a residence not to be changed.
Although there is cause to apprehend that accommodations are not now
so complete as might be wished, yet there is great reason to believe that
this inconvenience will cease with the present session.

It would be unbecoming the representatives of this nation to assemble
for the first time in this solemn temple without looking up to the Supreme
Ruler of the Universe and imploring His blessing.

May this territory be the residence of virtue and happiness! In this
city may that piety and virtue, that wisdom and magananimity, that con-
stancy and self-government, which adorned the great character whose
name it bears be forever held in veneration! Here and throughout our
country may simple manners, pure morals, and true religion flourish
forever!

It is with you, gentlemen, to consider whether the local powers over
the District of Columbia vested by the Constitution in the Congress of
the United States shall be immediately exercised. If in your opinion
this important trust ought now to be executed, you can not fail while
performing it to take into view the future probable situation of the territory for the happiness of which you are about to provide. You will
consider it as the capital of a great nation advancing with unexampled
rapidity in arts, in commerce, in wealth, and in population, and possess-
ing within itself those energies and resources which, if not thrown away
or lamentably misdirected, will secure to it a long course of prosperity
and self-government.

In compliance with a law of the last session of Congress, the officers and soldiers of the temporary army have been discharged. It affords real pleasure to recollect the honorable testimony they gave of the patriotic motives which brought them into the service of their country, by the readiness and regularity with which they returned to the station of private citizens.

It is in every point of view of such primary importance to carry the laws into prompt and faithful execution, and to render that part of the administration of justice which the Constitution and laws devolve on the Federal courts as convenient to the people as may consist with their present circumstances, that I can not omit once more to recommend to your serious consideration the judiciary system of the United States. No subject is more interesting than this to the public happiness, and to none can those improvements which may have been suggested by experience be more beneficially applied.

A treaty of amity and commerce with the King of Prussia has been concluded and ratified. The ratifications have been exchanged, and I have directed the treaty to be promulgated by proclamation.

The difficulties which suspended the execution of the sixth article of our treaty of amity, commerce, and navigation with Great Britain have not yet been removed. The negotiation on this subject is still depending. As it must be for the interest and honor of both nations to adjust this difference with good faith, I indulge confidently the expectation that the sincere endeavors of the Government of the United States to bring it to an amicable termination will not be disappointed.

The envoys extraordinary and ministers plenipotentiary from the United States to France were received by the First Consul with the respect due to their character, and three persons with equal powers were appointed to treat with them. Although at the date of the last official intelligence the negotiation had not terminated, yet it is to be hoped that our efforts to effect an accommodation will at length meet with a success proportioned to the sincerity with which they have been so often repeated.

While our best endeavors for the preservation of harmony with all nations will continue to be used, the experience of the world and our own experience admonish us of the insecurity of trusting too confidently to their success. We can not, without committing a dangeous imprudence, abandon those measures of self-protection which are adapted to our situation and to which, notwithstanding our pacific policy, the violence and injustice of others may again compel us to resort. While our vast extent of seacoast, the commercial and agricultural habits of our people, the great capital they will continue to trust on the ocean, suggest the system of defense which will be most beneficial to ourselves, our distance from Europe and our resources for maritime strength will enable us to employ it with effect. Seasonable and systematic arrangements, so far as our resources will justify, for a navy adapted to defensive war, and which may in case of necessity be quickly brought into use, seem to be as much recommended by a wise and true economy as by a just regard for our future tranquillity, for the safety of our shores, and for the protection of our property committed to the ocean.

The present Navy of the United States, called suddenly into existence by a great national exigency, has raised us in our own esteem, and by the protection afforded to our commerce has effected to the extent of our expectations the objects for which it was created.

In connection with a navy ought to be contemplated the fortification of some of our principal seaports and harbors. A variety of considerations, which will readily suggest themselves, urge an attention to this measure of precaution. To give security to our principal ports considerable sums have already been expended, but the works remain incomplete. It is for Congress to determine whether additional appropriations shall be made in order to render competent to the intended purposes the fortifications which have been commenced.

The manufacture of arms within the United States still invites the attention of the National Legislature. At a considerable expense to the public this manufacture has been brought to such a state of maturity as, with continued encouragement, will supersede the necessity of future importations from foreign countries.

Gentlemen of the House of Representatives:

I shall direct the estimates of the appropriations necessary for the ensuing year, together with an account of the public revenue and expenditure to a late period, to be laid before you. I observe with much satisfaction that the product of the revenue during the present year has been more considerable than during any former equal period. This result affords conclusive evidence of the great resources of this country and of the wisdom and efficiency of the measures which have been adopted by Congress for the protection of commerce and preservation of public credit.

Gentlemen of the Senate and Gentlemen of the House of Representatives:

As one of the grand community of nations, our attention is irresistibly drawn to the important scenes which surround us. If they have exhibited an uncommon portion of calamity, it is the province of humanity to deplore and of wisdom to avoid the causes which may have produced it. If, turing our eyes homeward, we find reason to rejoice at the prospect which presents itself; if we perceive the interior of our country prosperous, free, and happy; if all enjoy in safety, under the protection of laws emanating only from the general will, the fruits of their own labor, we ought to fortify and cling to those institutions which have been the source of such real felicity and resist with unabating perseverance the progress of those dangerous innovations which may diminish their influence.

To your patriotism, gentlemen, has been confided the honorable duty of guarding the public interests; and while the past is to your country a sure pledge that it will be faithfully discharged, permit me to assure you that your labors to promote the general happiness will receive from me the most zealous cooperation.

JOHN ADAMS.

BIBLIOGRAPHICAL AIDS

The emphasis in this and subsequent volumes in the **Presidential Chronologies** series will be on the administrations of the presidents. The more important works on other aspects of their lives, either before or after their terms in office, are included since they may contribute to an understanding of the presidential careers.

The following bibliography is critically selected. Many additional titles may be found in the works by Bowen, Kurtz, and Smith (see Biographies below) and in the standard guide. The student might also wish to consult **Reader's Guide to Periodical Literature** and **Social Sciences and Humanities Index** (formerly **International Index**) for recent articles in scholarly journals.

Additional chronological information not included in this volume because it did not relate directly to the president may be found in the **Encyclopedia of American History,** edited by Richard B. Morris, revised edition (New York, 1965).

Asterisks after titles refer to books currently available in paperback editions.

SOURCE MATERIALS

When the original edition of the **Diary and Autobiography of John Adams** (see **The Adams Papers** below) appeared in 1961 a review of them for the **American Historical Review** for January, 1963 was written by then President John F. Kennedy.

The importance of the publication so illustrated is the story of a vast amount of source material long hidden from the public view. Until 1902 the Adams papers, comprising the records of three major American statesmen, John Adams, John Quincy Adams, and Charles Francis Adams had been kept in the Stone Library in Quincy, Massachusetts under the personal charge of Charles Francis' sons. Then a trust was set up and the archives moved to the Massachusetts Historical Society in Boston. But the papers remained behind locked doors with access to them almost entirely denied by the trustees, fifth generation of the Adams family.

In 1952 a new generation, represented by Thomas Boylston Adams and John Quincy Adams, great-grandsons of Charles Francis Adams, decided to open the papers to historians and history. The entire collection was put on microfilm, 608 reels, and plans were made to begin publishing important parts of the collection covering the Adams Family to 1889. **The Diary and Autobiography of John Adams** is the first of this projected series which will eventually cover diaries of John Quincy Adams (perhaps twenty-four volumes) and Charles Francis Adams (some eighteen volumes) as well as journals, letters, papers, publications, and other relevant material. The complete collection is probably too vast to put into book form, and now and in the future only the microfilm edition will be the complete version. This is available only in the largest libraries.

The story of the Adams papers, past, present, and future, is interestingly told by Lyman H. Butterfield in the introduction to **The John Adams Papers,** Volume I.

The source materials below are only those which apply to John Adams, particularly those related to his presidency.

Adams, Charles Francis, ed. **Works of John Adams with a Life of the Author.** 10 vols. Boston, 1850-1856. Begun by John Quincy Adams, who abandoned the task after two chapters, this was the chief source for John Adams until 1952. The first volume is a biography, completed by Charles Francis Adams, and the other nine volumes combine Adams' incomplete diary and autobiography with some of his other writing, letters, and official papers. While good for its time, it is, from modern standards, incomplete and selective.

––––, ed. **Letters of John Adams Addressed to his Wife.** 2 vols. Boston, 1841. This, with a collection of letters from Abigail published the year before, and a volume of "Familiar Letters" of both published in 1876 are the present available printed sources of their correspondence. Series II, the "Adams Family Correspondence" of **The Adams Papers** is soon to be published.

Butterfield, Lyman H., ed. **The Adams Papers: Diary and Autobiography of John Adams.** 4 vols. Cambridge, 1961.*

––––, ed. **The Adams Papers: Adams Family Correspondence.** (December, 1761-March, 1778). 2 vols. Cambridge, 1963.

––––, ed. **The Adams Papers: The Earliest Diary of John Adams (June 1754-April 1754, September 1758-January 1759).** Cambridge, 1966. These are the first letter-press editions of **The Adams Papers.** They are unfortunately not of much value in the study of the administration of John Adams since Adams apparently kept no diary during his presidential term and his autobiography only goes to 1780. These volumes are, however, an excellent source in judging Adams as a person.

Koch, Adrienne and Peden, William, eds. **Selecting writings of John and John Quincy Adams.** New York, 1946. Contains some useful material.

Mitchell, Stewart, ed. **New Letters of Abigail Adams, 1788-1801.** Boston, 1947. These letters, written to her sister, Mary Cranch, add some interesting insights.

Peek, George A., Jr. **Political Writings of John Adams.** New York, 1954.* A short selection.

Wroth, L. Kinvin and Zobel, Hiller B., eds. **Legal Papers of John Adams.** 3 vols. Cambridge, 1965. Excellent research material for Adams' legal career, including the Writs of Assistance Case and the Boston Massacre trial.

BIOGRAPHIES

Bowen, Catherine Drinker. **John Adams and the American Resolution.** Boston, 1950*. This is "popular" or "fictionalized" biography at its best. Unfortunately, Mrs. Bowen's account ends in 1776 and one can get insights only into the earlier Adams and his environment.

Chinard, Gilbert. **Honest John Adams.** Boston, 1933.* Although now dated the Chinard biography is still a good treatment of Adams' entire career, with the possible exception of his early years for which Chinard did not have access to the materials now available. Particularly useful for understanding Adams' political philosophy.

Smith, Page. **John Adams.** 2 vols. New York, 1962. The first, and so far only, full-scale biography of John Adams published since the opening of the Adams papers to scholars in 1952. Some critics feel that there may have been too much exposure to the papers, with the inclusion of considerable trivial material. To fully understand the role of Adams as a president the student, while finding Smith's treatment valuable for the sequence of events, may wish to use some of the specialized treatments such as those by Dauer and Howe listed below.

ESSAYS

The student interested in the Administration of John Adams and who may start his investigation in one of the major encyclopedias will be disappointed. Each devotes only one paragraph to Adams' term in office. The bibliographical suggestions are also out of date.

The essay by W.C. Ford in the **Dictionary of American Biography** is more complete but devoted almost entirely to foreign policy. New interpretations are likely to be forthcoming and the student should consult **Reader's Guide to Periodical Literature** and **Social Sciences and Humanities Index** for any new treatments in scholarly journals. Recommended:

Kurtz, Stephen G. "John Adams," in **America's Ten Greatest Presidents.** Edited by Morton Borden (Chicago, 1961)*, 31-56.

White, Leonard D. "The Duty to Consult" and "The Hamilton-Adams Feud," chapters 4 and 20 in **The Federalists** (New York, 1948)*, 41-49 and 237-252.

MONOGRAPHS AND SPECIAL AREAS

Dauer, Manning, J. **The Adams Federalists.** Baltimore, 1953. An extremely valuable book which applies social science methodology to attempt to analyze the differences between the Adams and the Hamilton political and economic thought. Contains voting charts and similar other materials. The student might wonder whether Dauer's treatment tends to ignore the possibility of change or development in Adams' political philosophy as well as exaggerating "economic determinism." But, on the whole, a careful, well-documented study.

De Conde, Alexander. **The Quasi-War: The Politics and Diplomacy of the Undeclared War with France, 1797-1801.** New York, 1966. May be the definitive work on the most important issue in Adams' administration.

Green, Constance M. **Eli Whitney and the Birth of American Technology.** Boston, 1956. The often overlooked development of the concept of interchangeable parts, developed by Whitney during the Adams period.

Haraszti, Zoltan. **John Adams and the Prophets of Progress.** Cambridge, 1952.* A study of the intellectual and political history of the eighteenth century based on the marginal notes made by Adams in the books in his library. This could have been classified as source material but the editorial comments are a study in themselves.

Howe, John R., Jr. **The Changing Political Thought of John Adams.** Princeton, 1966. Defends the view that the John Adams of the 1790's, and thus as President, had changed his political views from those expressed in earlier writings. Scholarly and convincing.

Iacuzzi, Alfred. **John Adams, Scholar.** New York, 1952.

Kurtz, Stephen G. **The Presidency of John Adams: The Collapse of Federalism, 1795-1800.** Philadelphia, 1957.* In many ways this account of the Adams administration may leave the student unsatisfied. The organization and chronological treatment is somewhat confusing, and too much attention seems to be paid to Adams' opponents in his own party without enough attention to Adams' own actions or philosophy.

Miller, John C. **Crisis in Freedom: The Alien and Sedition Laws.** Boston, 1951.* A good treatment appearing in the McCarthy era.

Smith, James Morton. **Freedom's Fetters: The Alien and Sedition Laws and American Civil Liberties.** Ithaca, 1956. A definitive work which tends to assume that the Sedition Act was unconstitutional, a thesis challenged by some historians.

THE FEDERALIST ERA

Dorfman, Joseph. **The Economic Mind in American Civilization.** 4 vols. New York, 1946-1959. Important for an understanding of the period.

Kirk, Russell. **The Conservative Mind.** Chicago, 1953.* Useful for insights on John Adams' views.

Koch, Adrienne. **Jefferson and Madison: The Great Collaborators.** New York, 1950.* Good account of the origins of the Kentucky and Virginia Resolutions.

Malone, Dumas. **Jefferson and the Ordeal of Liberty.** Boston, 1962. Volume III of Malone's **Jefferson and His Time** includes the period of his Vice-Presidency, 1797-1801.

Miller, John C. **Alexander Hamilton: Portrait in Paradox.** New York, 1959.* Generally favorable.

————. **The Federalist Era, 1789-1801.** New York, 1960.* Contains a superb bibliography.

Schachner, James. **Alexander Hamilton.** New York, 1946.* A balanced view.

————. **The Founding Fathers.** New York, 1954.* A good account of the administrations of Washington and Adams.

White, Leonard D. **The Federalists, 1789-1801.** New York, 1948.* Valuable study of administrative precedents and procedures.

THE PRESIDENCY

Bailey, Thomas A. **Presidential Greatness: The Image and the Man from George Washington to the Present.** New York, 1966.* A critical and subjective study of the qualities of presidential greatness, arranged topically rather than chronologically. Bailey lists forty-three yardsticks for measuring presidential ability, and disagrees with the ranking given Adams in the Schlesinger poll of "Near Great" and instead rates him as "no higher than Below Average." The book includes an excellent up to date bibliography on presidential powers and problems, with special emphasis on measuring effectiveness or greatness according to the Bailey criteria.

Binkley, Wilfred E. **The Man in the White House: His Powers and Duties.** Revised ed. New York, 1964. Treats the development of the various roles of the American president.

Brown, Stuart Gerry. **The American Presidency: Leadership, Partisanship, and Popularity.** New York, 1966. Seeems to like the more partisan presidents like Jefferson and Jackson.

Corwin, Edward S. **The President: Office and Powers.** 4th ed. New York, 1957. An older classic.

Kane, Joseph Nathan. **Facts About the Presidents.** New York, 1959. Includes comparative as well as biographical data about the presidents.

Koenig, Louis W. **The Chief Executive.** New York, 1964. Authoritative study of presidential powers.

Laski, Harold J. **The American Presidency.** New York, 1940. A classic.

Rossiter, Clinton. **The American Presidency.** 2nd ed. New York, 1960. Useful.

Schlesinger, Arthur Meier. "Historians Rate United States Presidents," **Life,** XXV (November 1, 1948), 65 ff.

————. "Our Presidents: A Rating by Seventy-five Historians," **New York Times Magazine,** July 29, 1962, 12 ff.

NAME INDEX

Adams, Abigail Smith, wife, 2, 8, 9, 10, 12, 13, 14, 16, 17, 18
  see also Smith, Abigail
Adams, Abigail, daughter, 2, 8, 9
  see also Smith, Abigail Adams
Adams, Charles, son, 3, 7, 17
Adams, John, father, 1, 2
Adams, John Quincy, son, 2, 3, 6, 7, 8, 11, 12, 17, 18, 19
Adams, Joseph, great-grandfather, 2
Adams, Louisa Catherine Johnson, 18
  see also Johnson, Louisa Catherine
Adams, Samuel, 2, 4
Adams, Susanna, daughter, 3
Adams, Susanna Boylston, mother, 1
  see also Hall, Susanna Adams
Adams, Thomas Boylston, son, 3

Bache, Benjamin Franklin, 11, 14
Barclay, Hugh, 17
Barry, John, 11
Belcher, Mrs., 1
Burr, Aaron, 10, 17

Cleverly, Joseph, 1
Clinton, George, 10
Cooper, Thomas, 16
Corbet, Michael, 3
Cushing, Thomas, 4

Davie, William, R., 15, 16
Deane, Silas, 6, 7
Dexter, Samuel, 16
Dickinson, John, 4

Ellsworth, Oliver, 10, 15, 16

Fenno, John, 10
Franklin, Benjamin, 5, 6, 7, 8, 9, 11
Fries, John, 15

Gage, Thomas, 4
Gallatin, Albert, 12
George III, King, 2, 8, 9
Gerry, Elbridge, 11, 14
Giles, William Branch, 12

Habersham, Joseph, 10
Hall, Susanna (Boylston) Adams, mother, 11
  see also Adams, Susanna Boylston
Hamilton, Alexander, 12, 13, 14, 15, 17
Hancock, John, 3, 4
Harper, Robert Goodloe, 13
Henry, Patrick, 15
Hopkinson, Joseph, 13
Howe, Lord, 6
Hutchinson, Thomas, 4

Jay, John, 7, 8
Jefferson, Thomas, 5, 7, 8, 9, 10, 12, 14, 17, 18, 19
Johnson, Louisa Catherine, 11
  see also Adams, Louisa Catherine

Knox, Henry, 13, 14

Laurens, Henry, 7
Lee, Arthur, 6, 7
Lee, Charles, 10
Lee, Richard Henry, 5, 6
Livingston, Robert, 5, 8
Logan, George, 15
Louis XVI, King, 6

Maccarty, Thaddeus, 1
McHenry, James, 10, 12, 14, 16
Madison, James, 12, 15
Marbury, William, 17
Marsh, Joseph, 1
Marshall, John, 11, 16, 17
Monroe, James, 12, 18
Morris, Robert, 16
Murray, William Vans, 15, 16

Napoleon, 16, 17
Nickerson, Ansell, 3

Otis, James, 2
Oswald, Richard, 8

87